MW01250780

PRACTICE BOOK

TABLE OF CONTENTS

HEMISPHERES AND CONTINENTS ON THE GLOBE

Use the pictures of the globes below to complete the activities. For help, you can refer to pages G4–G11 in your textbook.

MAP A	MAP B
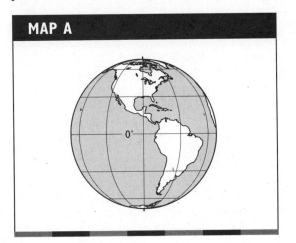	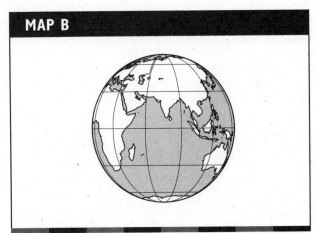

Map A: _____

1. Label the hemisphere for each map in the space provided.

2. In which hemisphere are the continents of North and South America located? Label them.

   _____

3. In which hemisphere are the continents of Africa, Asia, Europe, and Australia located? Label them.

   _____

4. Where would you place Antarctica? Label it.

   _____

   _____

5. Label the equator on both maps. Into which two hemispheres does the equator divide Earth?

   _____

   _____

Map B: _____

6. Label the following oceans on both maps.

   Atlantic Ocean   Pacific Ocean

   Indian Ocean   Arctic Ocean

7. Which continents are located in the Northern, Southern, and Eastern hemispheres?

   _____

8. Which continents are located in both the Western and Northern hemispheres?

   _____

   _____

9. What is the difference between lines of longitude and latitude?

   _____

   _____

   _____

FOLLOWING A TRIP TO FLORIDA ON A MAP

Use the map and map scale below to complete the activities. For help,
you can refer to pages G4–G11 in your textbook.

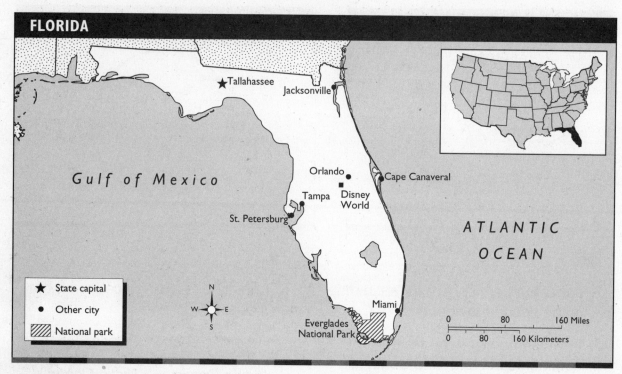

1. Mia and her family visited Florida.
In which part of the United States is
Florida?

_____

2. In Tampa the family rented a car
and drove to Disney World, near
Orlando. In which direction did they
travel?

_____

About how many miles did they
travel?

_____

3. After Disney World, they drove to
Cape Canaveral. In which direction
did they travel?

_____

4. About how many kilometers is
Cape Canaveral from Orlando?

_____

5. From Cape Canaveral, Mia and her
family drove to Miami. About how
many miles is Miami from Cape
Canaveral?

_____

6. Their friends took them to
Everglades National Park. In which
direction is the park from Miami?

_____

7. Then they flew from Miami to
St. Petersburg. In which direction
is St. Petersburg from Miami?

_____

USING A MAP TO EXPLORE CALIFORNIA

Use the map and map key on the right to complete the activities. For help, you can refer to pages G4–G11 in your textbook.

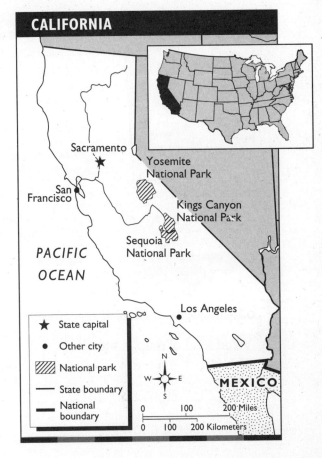

1. Jason lives in California. In which part of the country is the state located? Circle your answer.

   north   south   east   west

   What did you use to find the answer to the question above?

   _____

   _____

2. Jason lives in the state capital of California. Circle it on the map.

   How did you know which city was the state capital?

   _____

   _____

3. When he visits Mexico, Jason crosses a boundary. Circle the type of boundary he crosses.

   ━━━━━━━━━   ━━━━━━━━━

   What type of boundary is it?

   _____

4. Jason likes to visit California's national parks. His favorite is Yosemite National Park. In which direction is Yosemite National Park from Sacramento?

   _____

5. What two other national parks are located southeast of Yosemite?

   _____

6. What helped you locate these parks on the map?

   _____

USING A POLITICAL MAP OF THE SOUTHWEST

Use the map below to complete the activities. For help, you can refer to pages G4–G11 in your textbook.

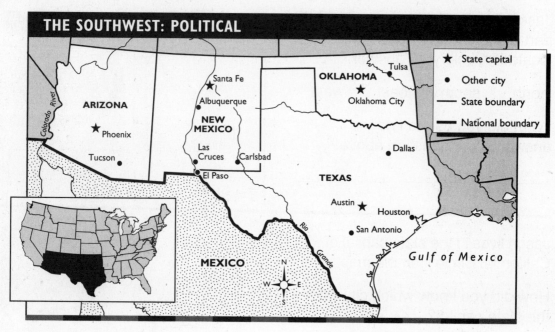

1. **a.** What kind of map is the one above?

    _____

    b. What does it show?

    _____

    _____

    _____

2. Which states are shown in the subject area of the map?

    _____

    _____

3. Name the states that are located on the national boundary line.

    _____

    _____

    _____

4. Which city on the map is located on the border of the United States and Mexico?

    _____

    _____

5. List the capital cities for the states shown on the map.

    _____

    _____

    _____

    _____

6. Which river runs along the national boundary line?

    _____

    _____

    _____

McGraw-Hill School Division

ROAD AND PHYSICAL MAPS OF COLORADO

Use the two maps of Colorado below to complete the activities. For help, you can refer to pages G4–G11 in your textbook.

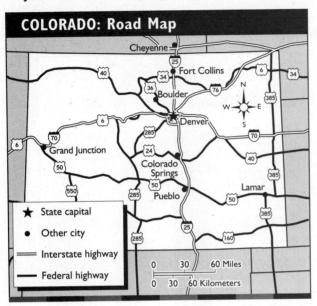

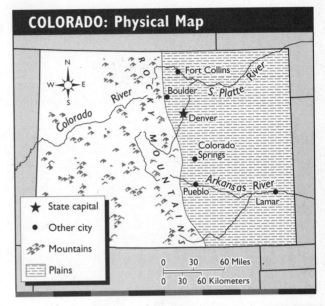

1. Which map would you use to plan a car trip through the state of Colorado?

_____

2. Which map would you use to find the location of the Rocky Mountains in Colorado?

_____

3. Which highway crosses Colorado from north to south?

_____

4. As you travel across Colorado from east to west, does the land become more or less mountainous?

_____

5. If you had to travel from Lamar to Pueblo, what highway would you take?

_____

6. Would you expect to be driving through mountains? Why or why not?

_____

_____

7. Suppose you and your family planned the trip described below. Name the highways you would take. Then trace the route in red on one of the maps.

a. From Pueblo you drive across the Rocky Mountains to Grand Junction.

_____

b. From Grand Junction you drive to Denver.

_____

TAKING A LOOK AT IMMIGRATION

Use the graphs below to complete the activities on this page. For help, you can refer to pages 8–11 in your textbook.

Immigration to the United States

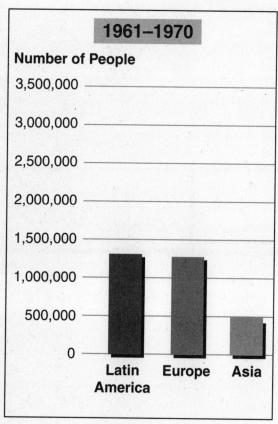

1961–1970

Number of People

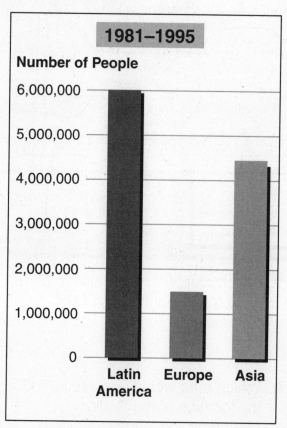

1981–1995

Number of People

Source: U.S. Census Bureau

1. What parts of the world are represented in the graphs?

   _____

   _____

   _____

2. Where did the fewest immigrants come from between 1961 and 1970?

   _____

3. From which part of the world did the most United States immigrants come in the years 1981 to 1995?

   _____

4. Name three places Latin American immigrants may come from.

   _____

   _____

   _____

THINKING ABOUT OUR GOVERNMENT

Read the paragraph below. Then answer the questions. For help, you can refer to pages 12–15 in your textbook.

We the People of the United States, in order to form a more perfect Union, establish justice, insure domestic tranquility, provide for the common defense, promote the general welfare, and secure the blessings of liberty to ourselves and our posterity, do ordain and establish this Constitution for the United States of America.

1. In what document can the paragraph above be found?

_____

2. What is this document a plan for?

_____

_____

3. What kind of government did this document set up for our country?

_____

_____

4. Which words show that the founders believed in democracy?

_____

_____

5. What is the role of the people in a democracy?

_____

_____

6. How do American citizens choose the people they want in government?

_____

7. What are the three levels of government for which American citizens choose representatives?

_____

_____

_____

8. The Constitution protects the individual rights of people living in the United States. What are these rights called?

_____

Give two examples of these rights.

_____

_____

DECISION MAKING

Rob's class is studying the history of local Native Americans. His teacher has given the class three choices for a class trip. Tomorrow they will vote on where to go. Read how Rob decided which trip to vote for. Then answer the questions. For help, you can refer to pages 16–17 in your textbook.

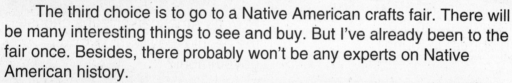

The first choice is to go to a local Native American village. I could see how local Native Americans once lived. I could speak with Native Americans about their history.

Our second choice is to go to the natural history museum. They have many Native American displays. But there wouldn't be any Native Americans to talk to about their history. Only a few displays would be about local Native Americans.

The third choice is to go to a Native American crafts fair. There will be many interesting things to see and buy. But I've already been to the fair once. Besides, there probably won't be any experts on Native American history.

The more I think about it, the better the Native American village sounds. I can learn about Native American history from the people themselves. Everything there will be about local Native Americans.

1. What decision did Rob have to make? _____

2. What was his goal? _____

3. Which two things didn't Rob consider as he thought about his decision? Put an **X** next to each one.

   _____ **a.** Talking to Native Americans about their history.

   _____ **b.** How much time it would take to get to each place.

   _____ **c.** How much each trip was going to cost.

4. Do you think Rob made a good decision? Why or why not?

   _____

   _____

   _____

IDENTIFYING SOURCES

Use the paragraphs on the right to complete the activities on this page. For help, you can refer to pages 18–21 in your textbook.

1. a. This paragraph is from a textbook written in 1986. The authors describe how immigrants to the United States in the late 1800s gathered in ethnic neighborhoods in big cities. Is the paragraph from a primary source or a secondary source?

_____

In cities such as Chicago they [immigrants] formed ethnic and national neighborhoods. When the Poles settled in Chicago, an area called "Little Poland" appeared. When Chinese people settled in San Francisco, "Chinatown" appeared. In New York City, Italians created "Little Italy" on Mulberry Street. Jewish families from Eastern Europe gathered together in New York's Lower East Side.

John Patrick and Carol Berkin, *History of the American Nation from 1877*, Vol. 2 (New York: Macmillan, 1986), page 511.

b. How do you know?

_____

_____

2. a. This quote is from an interview of Yusef Arbeely by a reporter in 1881. The reporter asked Arbeely how he and his family felt about immigrating to the United States from Damascus, Syria. Is the quote from a primary or a secondary source?

_____

The change from Damascus, almost the oldest city in the world, to this, the newest and most active civilization in the world, was very great. But I have not been disappointed. I left my relatives and friends behind because I desired freedom of speech and action and educational advantages for my children. In coming here I have escaped the disadvantages of a . . . tyrannical government, and have found all that I came in search of.

b. How do you know?

_____

_____

_____

_____

John Patrick and Carol Berkin, *History of the American Nation from 1877*, Vol. 2 (New York: Macmillan, 1986), page 30.

3. Why is it important to look at the history of our country's people?

_____

_____

_____

McGraw-Hill School Division

MATCHING WORDS AND THEIR MEANINGS

Match each term in the box with its meaning. For help, you can refer to the lessons in Chapter 1 of your textbook.

a. unity	**f.** culture	**k.** Constitution	**p.** ancestor
b. prejudice	**g.** primary source	**l.** immigrant	**q.** perspective
c. republic	**h.** ethnic group	**m.** secondary source	**r.** values
d. citizen	**i.** population	**n.** democracy	**s.** history
e. oral history	**j.** historian	**o.** civil rights	**t.** diversity

_____ **1.** an opinion made without proof

_____ **2.** the story of what happened in the past

_____ **3.** the individual rights of a citizen under the law

_____ **4.** a relative who lived before someone

_____ **5.** an account of the past given by someone who was not an eyewitness

_____ **6.** a group of people who share the same customs, the same language, and often the same history

_____ **7.** a person who is born in a country or who chooses to become a member of that country by law

_____ **8.** the customs, beliefs, and language of a people

_____ **9.** spoken records

_____ **10.** the beliefs that guide the way people live

_____ **11.** a government in which people create the laws and run the government

_____ **12.** the number of people living in a place

_____ **13.** information that comes directly from a time in the past

_____ **14.** the plan of government for our country

_____ **15.** being as one or being in agreement

_____ **16.** a person who studies the past

_____ **17.** a government in which people elect representatives to run the country

_____ **18.** a person who leaves one country to go and live in another land

_____ **19.** point of view

_____ **20.** many different cultures

LOOKING AT OUR COUNTRY'S REGIONS

Use the map to complete the activities on this page. For help, you can refer to pages 28–35 in your textbook.

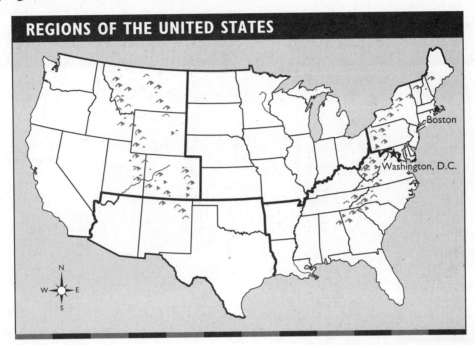

REGIONS OF THE UNITED STATES

Boston
Washington, D.C.

1. Use these words to label each region on the map.

   Southwest   Middle West

   Southeast   Northeast

   West

2. **a.** Color the Rocky Mountains brown. Then label them.

   b. In which region are they?

   _____

3. **a.** Use your pencil to shade the area that makes up the Corn Belt. Then label it.

   b. In which region is the Corn Belt?

   _____

4. **a.** Circle and label the Grand Canyon.

   b. In which region is this landform?

   _____

5. **a.** Color the Boswash area red. Then label it.

   b. In which region is the Boswash area?

   _____

6. **a.** Trace the Mississippi River in blue. Then label it.

   b. Through which two regions does this river flow?

   _____

   _____

McGraw-Hill School Division

COMPARING CLIMATE MAPS

Use these maps to help you answer the questions below. For help, you can refer to pages 36–39 in your textbook.

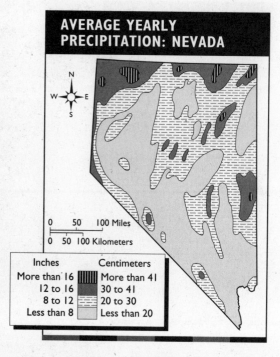

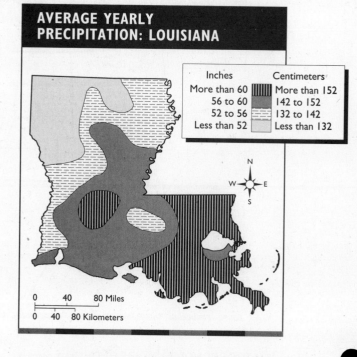

1. **What do the maps above show?**

    _____

    _____

    _____

2. **Is Nevada in Arid or Humid America? Explain.**

    _____

    _____

    _____

    _____

3. **Which part of Nevada receives the most precipitation?**

    _____

4. **Is Louisiana in Arid or Humid America? Explain.**

    _____

    _____

    _____

    _____

5. **Which part of Louisiana receives the least amount of precipitation?**

    _____

    _____

6. **How would you describe the difference in climate between Nevada and Louisiana?**

    _____

    _____

UNDERSTANDING LATITUDE AND LONGITUDE

Use the map below to complete the activities on this page. For help, you can refer to pages 40–41 in your textbook.

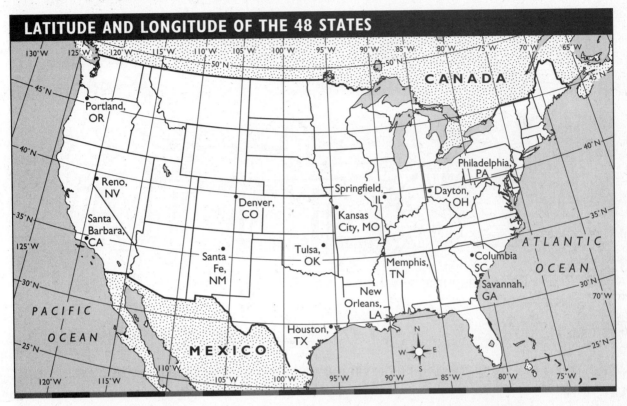

LATITUDE AND LONGITUDE OF THE 48 STATES

1. Liz and her family took a trip across the United States. They stopped at eight cities. Below are the latitude and longitude closest to each one. Find each city, then draw a line to show the route the family took.

first city:	45°N, 125°W	**fifth city:**	30°N, 90°W
second city:	35°N, 120°W	**sixth city:**	30°N, 80°W
third city:	35°N, 105°W	**seventh city:**	35°N, 80°W
fourth city:	30°N, 95°W	**eighth city:**	40°N, 75°W

2. On the way home Liz and her family stopped at the cities listed below. Find and circle each city on the map. Then write the lines of latitude and longitude that are closest to each city.

City	Latitude and Longitude
Springfield, Illinois	_____
Denver, Colorado	_____
Reno, Nevada	_____

USING OUR NATURAL RESOURCES

Use the picture below to complete the activities on this page. For help, you can refer to pages 42–48 in your textbook.

1. Which natural resource are these boys using as a material for their paper airplanes?

   _____

2. Name two other objects shown in the picture that are also made from this natural resource.

   _____

3. Is this natural resource a renewable or a nonrenewable resource? Explain.

   _____

   _____

4. List three benefits we get from this natural resource.

   _____

   _____

   _____

5. Name three other kinds of natural resources found in the United States.

   _____

6. What is conservation? _____

   _____

McGraw-Hill School Division

MATCHING WORDS AND THEIR MEANINGS

Match each term in the box with its meaning. Write the letter of the correct term next to each meaning. For help, you can refer to the lessons in Chapter 2 of your textbook.

a. recycle	**f.** climate	**k** natural resources	**p.** precipitation
b. humid	**g.** pollution	**l.** temperature	**q.** megalopolis
c. arid	**h.** fossil fuel	**m.** renewable resource	**r.** geography
d. mineral	**i.** acid rain	**n.** nonrenewable resource	**s.** economy
e. region	**j.** interdependent	**o.** environment	

_____ 1. the weather an area has over a number of years

_____ 2. the study of Earth and the way people live on it and use it

_____ 3. dry

_____ 4. all the surroundings in which people, plants, and animals live

_____ 5. a resource that can be replaced

_____ 6. polluted moisture that falls to the ground

_____ 7. a substance found in the earth that is neither plant nor animal

_____ 8. the measurement of heat and cold

_____ 9. dependent on each other to meet needs and wants

_____ 10. to use something again

_____ 11. materials found in nature that people use to meet their needs and wants

_____ 12. wet

_____ 13. the way people use natural resources, money, and knowledge to produce goods and services

_____ 14. a resource that cannot be replaced

_____ 15. a large area that has common features that set it apart from other areas

_____ 16. rain or snow

_____ 17. something that makes our air, soil, and water dirty

_____ 18. a fuel, such as oil, coal, or gas, formed over millions of years from fossils

_____ 19. a group of cities that have grown so close together they seem to form one city

McGraw-Hill School Division

Chapter 2, Vocabulary Review

LOOKING AT MAYA CULTURE

Use the pictures on the right to complete the activities on this page. For help, you can refer to pages 60–63 in your textbook.

1. **a.** Draw a line to the picture that shows part of an ancient Maya city.

   b. What is the stone building in the center called?

   _____

   c. In which present-day country is this city located?

   _____

2. **a.** Draw a line to the picture that shows an example of Maya writing.

   b. How does this writing differ from words written using an alphabet?

   _____

   _____

   _____

Tikal

   c. What invention helped make the Maya calendar correct?

   _____

   _____

3. **a.** Draw a line to the picture that shows a Maya monument.

   b. Who studies such monuments from the past?

   _____

   c. Why did the Maya build monuments like this?

   _____

   _____

McGraw-Hill School Division

EXPLORING TENOCHTITLÁN

Use the diagram to complete the activities below. For help, you can refer
to pages 64–69 in your textbook.

The Island City of Tenochtitlán

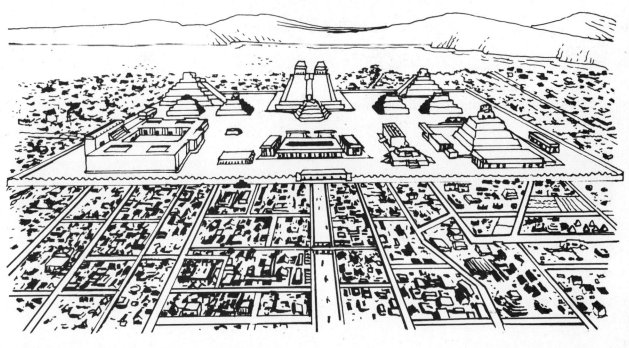

1. What empire had Tenochtitlán as its capital? _____

2. What were the Aztec honoring when they planned the city?

   _____

3. Circle the Great Temple. What was important about where this and
   other buildings were located in the city?

   _____

   _____

4. Describe how the Aztec culture was one of both great beauty and great cruelty.

   _____

   _____

   _____

   _____

TIME LINE OF MAYA HISTORY

Use the information in the time line to decide whether each sentence is true. Put an **X** next to each true sentence. For help, you can refer to pages 70–71 in your textbook.

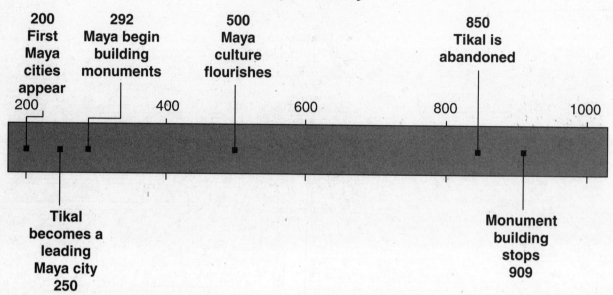

Maya History

_____ 1. This time line covers a time period of 800 years.

_____ 2. The first Maya cities appeared at the beginning of the third century, about 200 years after the birth of Christ.

_____ 3. Tikal was an important Maya city for about 600 years.

_____ 4. Maya monument building stopped about 900 years after it began.

_____ 5. The Maya culture flourished in the third century.

_____ 6. Tikal was abandoned around 850.

COMPARING EARLY NORTH AMERICAN CULTURES

Draw a line under the word or words that correctly complete each sentence. For help, you can refer to pages 72–77 in your textbook.

Great Serpent Mound

Mesa Verde

1. The people who built Cahokia are known as the _____.

   a. Pueblo　　c. Mound Builders

   b. Anasazi　　d. Maya

2. They lived in an area with _____.

   a. an arid climate

   b. cold temperatures all year

   c. plenty of rainfall

3. The mound pictured was built _____.

   a. from stones

   b. from piles of earth

   c. out of wood

4. This mound was used for _____.

   a. burying their dead

   b. the foundations of buildings

   c. protection from enemies

5. The people who built Mesa Verde are known as the _____.

   a. Pueblo　　c. Mound Builders

   b. Anasazi　　d. Maya

6. They lived in an area with _____.

   a. an arid climate

   b. cold temperatures all year

   c. plenty of rainfall

7. The village pictured was built _____.

   a. on a mound

   b. in a forest

   c. in the side of a cliff

8. A major problem these people overcame was _____.

   a. a lack of water

   b. attacks from enemies

   c. disease

McGraw-Hill School Division

USING NEW WORDS

Use a word from the box to complete each sentence. For help, you can refer to the lessons in Chapter 3 of your textbook.

archaeologist	slavery	irrigation	surplus	drought
civilization	artifact	specialize	tribute	empire

1. If you had more of something than you needed, you might say that you had a _____.

2. A large area of many peoples controlled by one ruler or government is an _____.

3. If you described a method by which water is brought into dry areas, you would be describing a system of _____.

4. People who spend most of their time doing one kind of job are people who _____.

5. To describe a culture with complex systems of government, education, and religion, you might use the word _____.

6. If you met a scientist who looks for and studies evidence from long ago, you would have met an _____.

7. If your payment to a leader took the form of valuable goods, you would be paying a _____.

8. A long period with very little rain is a _____.

9. If you found an object left behind by people who lived long ago, you would have found an _____.

10. If you described the practice of people owning other people and forcing them to work, you would be describing _____.

Chapter 3, Vocabulary Review

McGraw-Hill School Division

THINKING ABOUT THE TLINGIT

Use the picture below to complete the activities on this page. For help, you can refer to pages 82–87 in your textbook.

1. The picture shows the Tlingit as they might have looked long ago. Where were these Native Americans likely to have been living? Circle your answer.

   Northwest Coast   Southern California   Great Basin

2. Why was salmon an important resource for the Tlingit?

   _____

3. Circle two objects in the picture that are examples of Tlingit technology. What

   allowed the Tlingit to concentrate on developing their technology? _____

   _____

   _____

4. Draw a box around the object in the picture that took great skill to make. What

   is this object called and why were objects like this built? _____

   _____

   _____

5. How did the Tlingit and other Native Americans in the area preserve their culture after their homeland became part of the United States?

   _____

   _____

McGraw-Hill School Division

THINKING ABOUT HOPI LIFE

Use the pictures on the right to complete the activities on this page. For help, you can refer to pages 90–94 in your textbook.

1. a. Draw a line to the picture that shows how the Hopi used adobe.

   b. Why was adobe a good building material?

_____

_____

_____

Kachina ceremony

2. a. Draw a line to the picture that shows how the Hopi grew their crops.

   b. Why did the Hopi use this method of farming?

_____

_____

Dry farming

3. a. Draw a line to the picture that shows an important part of Hopi religion.

   b. Why are the kachinas important to the Hopi?

_____

_____

_____

_____

_____

Pueblo

McGraw-Hill School Division

Name: _____

TALKING WITH A LAKOTA SIOUX

If you had a chance to talk with Standing Bear, a Lakota Sioux, you might ask him questions similar to the ones below. Use the spaces to write the answers you think Standing Bear might give. For help, you can refer to pages 96–101 in your textbook.

Question: Standing Bear, in what part of the Great Plains do you live?

Standing Bear: _____

_____

Question: What are the land and climate like?

Standing Bear: _____

_____

Question: I know that large herds of buffalo roam the Great Plains. How does the buffalo play a part in the life of your people?

Standing Bear: _____

_____

Question: Why do you live in teepees?

Standing Bear: _____

_____

Question: You have horses. Where did the horses originally come from?

Standing Bear: _____

_____

Question: How did taming horses change the way of life for Native Americans living on the Great Plains?

Standing Bear: _____

_____

_____

_____

McGraw-Hill School Division

THE IROQUOIS OF THE EASTERN WOODLANDS

Use the map and your textbook to find out if the statements below are true or false. If a statement is true, write **True** after it. If a statement is false, write **False** after it. Then write the reasons for your answers. For help, you can refer to pages 102–107 in your textbook.

1. The Iroquois had many places to fish.

_____

_____

_____

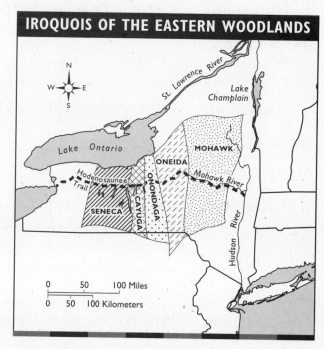

IROQUOIS OF THE EASTERN WOODLANDS

2. The Iroquois were the only Native Americans living in the Eastern Woodlands.

_____

_____

_____

3. The Hodenosaunee Trail connected the five major Iroquois peoples.

_____

_____

4. Women had very little power in the Iroquois world. _____

_____

_____

_____

5. Because the Iroquois were such poor warriors, they formed the Iroquois Confederacy in order to increase their strength. _____

_____

_____

McGraw-Hill School Division

UNDERSTANDING CAUSE AND EFFECT

Read the paragraph below. Then underline the correct answer to each question. For help, you can refer to pages 108–109 in your textbook.

When the Spanish explorers began arriving in North America in the 1500s, they brought many horses with them. Over the next hundred years, large numbers of these horses became wild. By the 1700s Native Americans such as the Lakota were taming these horses and adapting them to their way of life. Many Plains peoples became expert riders, trainers, and breeders. But the most important change horses brought to these peoples was in their economy. Because horses made travel faster and easier, Native Americans could follow the wanderings of the buffalo herds. As a result, hunting replaced farming as the main source of food. Many Plains peoples stopped living in permanent settlements. Instead, they began to move their villages from one campsite to another in order to follow the buffalo herds. As hunting buffalo became an important part of life, many Plains peoples began to depend on the buffalo for food, clothing, and shelter.

1. What is the main cause-and-effect connection in the paragraph?

   a. how the horse changed the way of life for the Plains peoples

   b. why the Spanish brought horses with them to North America

   c. what happens to horses when they are allowed to roam free

2. Why were Native Americans able to follow the buffalo herds?

   a. they gave up farming

   b. wild horses were roaming the plains

   c. horses made travel faster and easier

3. What word clue in the paragraph helped you answer question 2?

   a. because

   b. since

   c. as a result

4. Why is it important to understand cause-and-effect connections?

   _____

   _____

   _____

   _____

MATCHING WORDS AND THEIR MEANINGS

Write the letter of the term that matches each definition. For help, you can refer to the lessons in Chapter 4 of your textbook.

---

a. adobe   **e.** potlatch   **i.** coup stick   **m.** clan

b. lodge   **f.** longhouse   **j.** technology   **n.** prairie

c. teepee   **g.** wampum   **k.** compromise   **o.** travois

d. pueblo   **h.** totem pole   **l.** Iroquois Confederacy   **p.** jerky

                                                                    q. kachina

---

_____ **1.** the design and use of tools, ideas, and methods to solve problems

_____ **2.** a tall log carved with many designs

_____ **3.** a special Tlingit feast at which guests, not hosts, receive gifts

_____ **4.** a Spanish word that means "village"

_____ **5.** a type of clay found in the earth

_____ **6.** a spirit who the Hopi believe brings rain, helps crops grow, shows people how to live and behave, and brings peace and prosperity

_____ **7.** thin strips of dried meat

_____ **8.** a flat or gently rolling land covered mostly with grasses and wildflowers

_____ **9.** a cone-shaped tent made of animal skins

_____ **10.** a sled-like device used for transporting things

_____ **11.** a special weapon used by the Lakota to touch an enemy without killing him

_____ **12.** a home made of logs covered with grasses, sticks, and soil

_____ **13.** a long building made of poles covered with sheets of bark

_____ **14.** polished beads, usually made from shells, strung or woven together

_____ **15.** a group of families who share the same ancestor

_____ **16.** the union of five separate Iroquois peoples for a common purpose

_____ **17.** the settling of disputes by agreeing that each side will give up part of its demands

Chapter 4, Vocabulary Review

McGraw-Hill School Division

CHINESE EXPLORATION AND TRADE

Use the information in the box to make a chart of important events in Chinese exploration and trade. Then answer the questions that follow. The first event has been filled in for you. For additional help, refer to pages 114–117 in your textbook.

> - Zheng He begins the first of seven sea voyages to places outside the Chinese empire.
> - The Chinese push the Mongols out.
> - A new Chinese emperor orders that the empire's sailing ships be destroyed.
> - Mongols from northern Asia gain control of the Chinese empire.
> - Zhu Di orders the building of thousands of sailing ships.

CHART OF CHINESE EXPLORATION AND TRADE	
DATE	EVENT
late 1200s	Mongols from northern Asia gain control of the Chinese empire.
1368	
1403	
1405	
1525	

1. About how many years was it from the time the Chinese pushed the Mongols out until Zhu Di ordered the building of thousands of ships? _____

2. For about how many years was China a sea power? _____

3. Why was the Silk Road so important? _____

USING CIRCLE AND LINE GRAPHS

In the early 1400s China's rulers built a fleet of ships for exploring areas beyond China's borders. The graphs below show some facts about China's fleet. Use the graphs to complete these activities. Circle the answer to each question. For help, you can refer to pages 118–119 in your textbook.

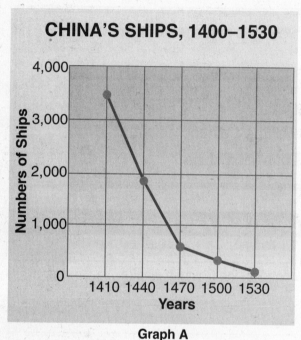

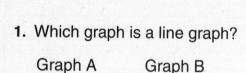

Graph A

Source: *When China Ruled the Seas,* by Louise Levathes, 1994

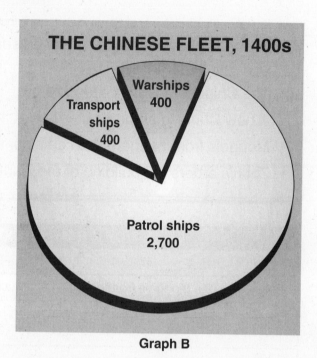

Graph B

Source: *When China Ruled the Seas,* by Louise Levathes, 1994

1. Which graph is a line graph?

   Graph A   Graph B

2. Which graph shows how many ships China had in 1500?

   Graph A   Graph B

3. Which shows each kind of ship the Chinese had in the early 1400s?

   Graph A   Graph B

4. In which year did China have the most ships?

   1410   1440   1470

   1500   1530

5. Which graph did you use to answer question 4?

   Graph A   Graph B

6. How many transport ships did the Chinese have in the early 1400s?

   400   2,700

7. Which graph did you use to answer question 6?

   Graph A   Graph B

8. How many ships were in the Chinese fleet in 1410?

   2,700   1,900   3,500

McGraw-Hill School Division

TRADE AND THE SONGHAI EMPIRE

Use the map to complete the activities below. For help, you can refer to pages 120–123 in your textbook.

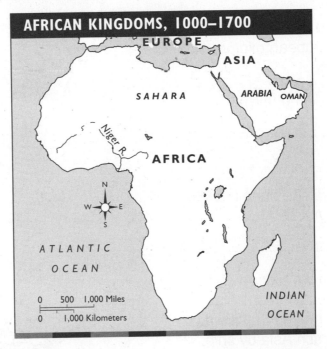

1. a. Outline the kingdom of Songhai in blue. Then label it.

   b. Who was king of Songhai in 1464?

   _____

   c. What city did he capture in 1468? In 1475?

   _____

   _____

2. a. Make a dot to show the location of each of the following cities. Then label each city.

   Gao   Timbuktu   Jenne

   b. Why were these cities important?

   _____

   _____

3. a. Draw one of the major caravan routes into and out of Songhai in red.

   b. List the parts of the world outside of Africa to which these trade routes led.

   _____

4. a. List two goods that Songhai traded.

   _____

   b. Where did these goods come from?

   _____

   _____

EARLY EUROPEAN EXPLORERS

Use the pictures on the right to help you complete the activities on this page. For help, you can refer to pages 124–127 in your textbook.

1. a. Draw a line to the picture of one of the first European explorers to travel to China.

   b. Which route did he take?

   _____

   _____

   c. What things did he bring back to Europe from Asia?

   _____

Prince Henry

2. a. Draw a line to the picture of the person whose inventions and technologies proved that it was possible to reach Asia by ship.

   b. Which route did his ships follow?

   _____

   _____

   c. Why did European traders want to find a sea route to Asia?

   _____

   _____

   _____

Vasco da Gama

3. a. Draw a line to the picture of the Portuguese explorer who finally reached Asia by ship.

   b. What did his voyage show European traders?

   _____

   _____

   _____

Marco Polo

McGraw-Hill School Division

FINDING AND USING NEW WORDS

Hidden among the letters in the box are words that match each definition that follows. The words may be read forward, backward, up, or down. Circle each word as you find it. Then write the word in the space before its definition. For help, you can refer to the lessons in Chapter 5 of your textbook.

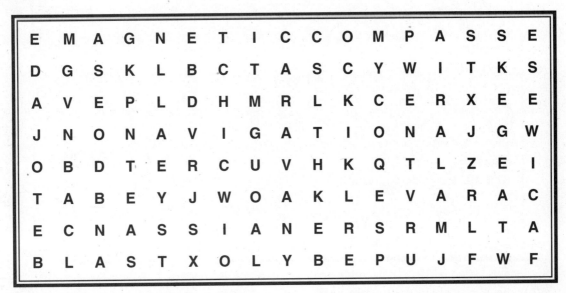

```
E  M  A  G  N  E  T  I  C  C  O  M  P  A  S  S  E
D  G  S  K  L  B  C  T  A  S  C  Y  W  I  T  K  S
A  V  E  P  L  D  H  M  R  L  K  C  E  R  X  E  E
J  N  O  N  A  V  I  G  A  T  I  O  N  A  J  G  W
O  B  D  T  E  R  C  U  H  K  Q  T  L  Z  E  I
T  A  B  E  Y  J  W  O  A  K  L  E  V  A  R  A  C
E  C  N  A  S  S  I  A  N  E  R  S  R  M  L  T  A
B  L  A  S  T  X  O  L  Y  B  E  P  U  J  F  W  F
```

_____ 1. a group of people traveling together, especially through desert areas

_____ 2. a disease caused by the bite of certain kinds of mosquitoes

_____ 3. a small ship that was fast and easy to steer, even in dangerous waters

_____ 4. a period of cultural and artistic growth that began in Italy in the 1300s

_____ 5. an instrument invented by the Chinese in about A.D. 100

_____ 6. the science of finding out a ship's direction and location

COLUMBUS'S EXPEDITIONS

Use the map on this page to complete the activities below. For help, you can refer to pages 138–145 in your textbook.

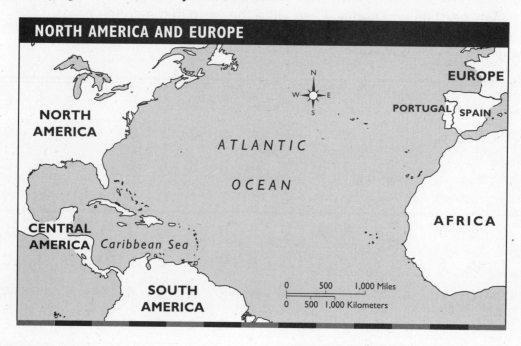

NORTH AMERICA AND EUROPE

1. Why did Columbus make his first expedition?

   _____

   _____

   _____

2. Locate the islands Columbus reached on his first expedition. Color them green and label them.

3. What did Columbus name the first island he visited in the Americas?

   _____

4. Draw the route of Columbus's first expedition in red.

5. What do historians call the movement of people, plants, animals, and germs that resulted from these expeditions?

   _____

6. What changes took place in the Eastern Hemisphere as a result of this exchange?

   _____

   _____

   _____

   _____

   _____

7. What changes took place in the Americas as a result of this exchange?

   _____

   _____

   _____

   _____

McGraw-Hill School Division

THE FALL OF TENOCHTITLÁN

Read the paragraph below. It is part of an account written about the religious center of Tenochtitlán by Hernando Cortés during his conquest of the Aztec. Then complete the activities. For additional background, refer to pages 148–153 in your textbook.

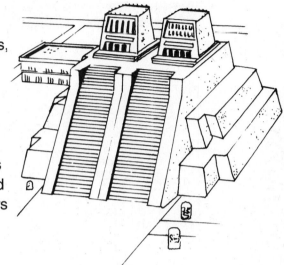

Inside . . . are fine buildings with large halls and corridors. There are at least 40 pyramids, very tall and well made; the largest has 50 steps leading up to the main body of the pyramid. . . . The stone masonry and the woodwork are equally good; they could nowhere be bettered. All the stonework inside the temples where they keep the idols is sculptured, and the woodwork is all carved in relief and painted with pictures of monsters and other figures and designs.

Editors, Time-Life Books, *Aztecs: Reign of Blood & Splendor* (Alexandria, VA: Time-Life Books, 1992).

1. How do you think Cortés felt about Tenochtitlán when he first saw it?

   _____

   _____

2. What was the name of the Aztec emperor at this time? _____

   What happened to him? _____

3. List two reasons why Cortés and his Spanish soldiers were able to conquer Tenochtitlán and the Aztec empire.

   _____

   _____

4. What happened to Tenochtitlán after it fell to Cortés?

   _____

   _____

5. What did the Spanish call their new colony? _____

6. What did Tenochtitlán become known as? _____

READING HISTORICAL MAPS

The historical map below shows the routes of some Spanish explorers in North America. Use the map to complete the activities on this page. For help, you can refer to pages 154–155 in your textbook.

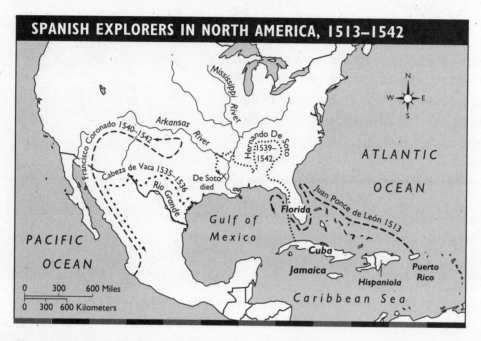

SPANISH EXPLORERS IN NORTH AMERICA, 1513–1542

1. List two clues that tell you this is a historical map.

   _____

   _____

   _____

2. List the names of the explorers whose routes are shown.

   _____

   _____

   _____

3. What major river did Hernando De Soto cross?

   _____

4. What part of North America did Francisco Coronado explore? Circle your answer.

   southeast   southwest

   northeast   northwest

5. During what years did Cabeza de Vaca explore Mexico?

   _____

6. What present-day state did Ponce de León explore, and in what year did he explore it?

   _____

   What island in the Caribbean Sea did he sail from?

   _____

LIFE IN NEW SPAIN

Look at each picture and read its caption. Then, in the space provided, tell what life was like in New Spain for the people shown in the picture. For help, you can refer to pages 156–161 in your textbook.

Indians at work on an encomienda

_____
_____
_____
_____
_____
_____
_____

Enslaved Africans loading a ship

_____
_____
_____
_____
_____

Spanish living in Mexico City

_____
_____
_____
_____
_____
_____

FINDING AND USING NEW WORDS

Find the term that is hidden in each group of letters. Write the term on the line.

1. Cross out these letters: d, e, f, g. _____

   e f c g d o l e f d o e n g y

2. Cross out these letters: g, l, p, s. _____

   s e n l c g o m p s l i e n g d s l a

3. Cross out these letters: a, b, c. _____

   a e x b c p e d a i t b i c o n a

4. Cross out these letters: d, e, g, u. _____

   d e m i g u s e d s i o d u g n d a r e u y

5. Cross out these letters: f, k, p. _____

   f C o k p l u p m b f i a k n e p x c h k a f n g p k e

6. Cross out these letters: b, e, w. _____

   c w e o n e b q e u i s e w t b a d e o w r

Write each term from above next to its meaning. For help, you can look back at Chapter 6 in your textbook.

_____ 7. a journey made for a special purpose

_____ 8. a settlement far away from the country that rules it

_____ 9. the movement of people, plants, animals, and germs across the Atlantic Ocean

_____ 10. a soldier who conquered new lands for Spain

_____ 11. a large piece of land granted by Spain to certain Spanish colonists

_____ 12. a person who teaches his or her religion to others who have different beliefs

THE "LOST COLONY"

Use the information in the box to make a chart of important events about Roanoke Island. Then answer the questions that follow. The first event has been filled in for you. For help, you can refer to pages 168–171 in your textbook.

> - Sir Walter Raleigh sends John White and a second group of colonists to Roanoke Island. That same year John White returns to England for supplies.
> - John White returns to Roanoke. All the colonists have vanished.
> - English settlers first come to Roanoke Island. They soon return to England.
> - John White is delayed in returning to Roanoke by England's war with Spain.

IMPORTANT EVENTS IN THE SETTLEMENT OF ROANOKE ISLAND	
DATE	EVENT
1585	English settlers first come to Roanoke Island. They soon return to England.
1587	
1588	
1590	

1. About how many years was it between the arrivals of the two groups of colonists on Roanoke Island? _____

2. Why was John White's return to Roanoke Island delayed? _____
_____

3. What do you think might have happened to the "lost colony"?
_____
_____
_____

McGraw-Hill School Division

TELLING FACT FROM OPINION

John White may have made statements similar to the ones below about the "lost colony" of Roanoke Island. Decide if each statement is a fact or an opinion. Circle your choice. Then explain your answer. For help, you can refer to pages 172–173 in your textbook.

1. I believed that Roanoke Island was an ideal place for England's first colony in North America.

fact   opinion

Explanation: _____

_____

_____

2. I landed at Roanoke Island in July 1587 with more than 100 men, women, and children.

fact   opinion

Explanation: _____

_____

3. I had to return to England in the same year because the colony's supplies were running low.

fact   opinion

Explanation: _____

_____

4. I reached England in November 1587, only to find the country preparing to fight the Spanish Armada.

fact   opinion

Explanation: _____

_____

5. It seemed to me that the English were better at fighting at sea than the Spanish.

fact   opinion

Explanation: _____

_____

6. I believed that the English fleet could easily outmaneuver the Spanish ships.

fact   opinion

Explanation: _____

_____

7. I returned to Roanoke in August 1590 to find that the colonists had vanished.

fact   opinion

Explanation: _____

_____

Chapter 7, Thinking Skills

McGraw-Hill School Division

SEARCHING FOR THE NORTHWEST PASSAGE

Use the map to complete the activities below. For help, you can refer to pages 174–177 in your textbook.

1. In 1609 Henry Hudson explored the coast of North America. He traveled north from present-day South Carolina. Label the two bays that Hudson saw.

2. Label New York Harbor.

3. Trace in blue the river Hudson sailed up. What is this river called today?

   _____

4. What was Hudson searching for?

   _____

   _____

5. Who paid for Hudson's expedition?

   _____

   _____

AREA OF HENRY HUDSON'S 1609 VOYAGE

NORTH AMERICA

ATLANTIC OCEAN

6. What was the company supposed to get in return for paying for the expedition?

   _____

   _____

7. Even though Hudson did not find what he was looking for, how did the Dutch benefit from his voyage?

   _____

   _____

8. What happened as a result of European exploration of North America's east coast?

   _____

   _____

McGraw-Hill School Division

Name: _____

LOOKING AT JAMESTOWN

Use the map to help you complete the activities below. For help, you can refer to pages 178–185 in your textbook.

1. What does the shaded area on the map show?

   _____

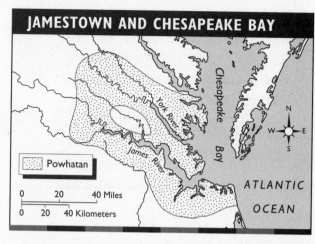

2. **a.** Locate and circle Jamestown.

   b. Why did the colonists settle here?

   _____

   _____

3. What hardships did the colonists encounter? _____

   _____

4. **a.** Who saved Jamestown? _____

   b. How did he save the colony? _____

   _____

5. How did tobacco change the colony?

   _____

   _____

   _____

6. List two other major events that helped the colony grow.

   _____

   _____

   _____

   _____

McGraw-Hill School Division

HEADLINES ABOUT PLYMOUTH

Below are headlines that might have appeared in the early 1600s. Each tells something that happened to the Pilgrims. Read and answer the questions. For help, you can refer to pages 186–191 in your textbook.

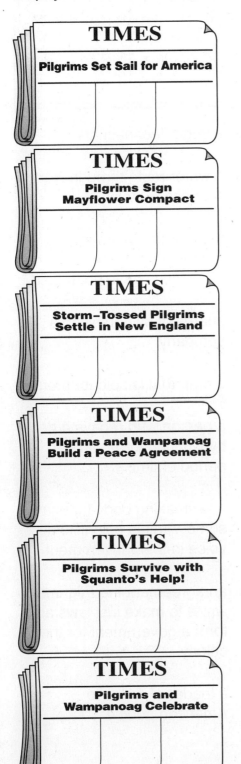

TIMES

Pilgrims Set Sail for America

TIMES

Pilgrims Sign
Mayflower Compact

TIMES

Storm-Tossed Pilgrims
Settle in New England

TIMES

Pilgrims and Wampanoag
Build a Peace Agreement

TIMES

Pilgrims Survive with
Squanto's Help!

TIMES

Pilgrims and
Wampanoag Celebrate

1. Why did the Pilgrims go to North America?

_____

_____

2. Why was the Mayflower Compact important?

_____

_____

3. Why did the Pilgrims settle in New England instead of Virginia?

_____

_____

4. With whom did the Pilgrims make a peace agreement?

_____

_____

5. How did Squanto help the Pilgrims survive?

_____

_____

6. Why did the Pilgrims and the Wampanoag celebrate?

_____

_____

What do we call this celebration today?

_____

USING NEW WORDS

Use the codes in the box to figure out the words. Then write the number of each word next to its meaning. For help, you can refer to Chapter 7 of your textbook.

a = 26	e = 24	i = 22	m = 20	q = 18	u = 16	y = 14
b = 1	f = 3	j = 5	n = 7	r = 9	v = 11	z = 13
c = 25	g = 23	k = 21	o = 19	s = 17	w = 15	
d = 2	h = 4	l = 6	p = 8	t = 10	x = 12	

1. 17 10 19 25 21

   _____

2. 25 26 17 4   25 9 19 8

   _____

3. 20 26 14 3 6 19 15 24 9
   25 19 20 8 26 25 10

   _____

4. 7 19 9 10 4 15 24 17 10
   8 26 17 17 26 23 24

   _____

5. 26 9 20 26 2 26

   _____

6. 4 19 16 17 24   19 3
   1 16 23 24 17 17 24 17

   _____

7. 17 26 25 4 24 20

   _____

8. 22 7 2 24 7 10 16 9 24 2
   17 24 9 11 26 7 10

   _____

9. 8 9 19 3 22 10

   _____

_____ a. a large fleet of ships

_____ b. a water route through North America to Asia

_____ c. the amount of money remaining after the costs of a business have been paid

_____ d. shares of ownership in a company

_____ e. a crop that is sold for money

_____ f. a person who repays a debt by working for an agreed period of time

_____ g. a lawmaking body that gave some Virginia colonists a voice in their government

_____ h. an agreement the Pilgrims wrote to make just laws and form a government for their colony

_____ i. a leader of a Native American people

Chapter 7, Vocabulary Review

McGraw-Hill School Division

Name: _____

SETTLING THE NEW ENGLAND COLONIES

Each person shown below played a part in settling the New England colonies. Write the correct words to complete the statements about each person. For help, you can refer to pages 204–209 in your textbook.

1. I was the leader of the _____.

   Like the Pilgrims, we decided to leave

   _____ in order to practice our

   _____ in peace. We founded the

   _____. Our first

   settlement was named _____.

John Winthrop

2. I believed that the colony needed to _____

   different religious beliefs. I fled Massachusetts and

   founded the settlement of _____

   in what then became _____.

   It was the first European colony to allow

   _____.

Roger Williams

3. I was brought to trial because I believed people should

   pray directly to _____ rather than

   depend upon church _____. I was

   forced to leave_____. I traveled to

   _____ and started the settlement

   of _____.

Anne Hutchinson

McGraw-Hill School Division

LOOKING AT THE MIDDLE COLONIES

Use the picture and words below to help you complete the activities on the page. For help, you can refer to pages 210–213 in your textbook.

I am very sensible of unkindness and injustice that hath been too much exercised toward you by the people of these parts of the world, but I am not such a man.

—William Penn

1. **a.** The picture shows William Penn meeting with a group of Native Americans. What was their name?

   _____

   b. Why were they meeting?

   _____

2. What did William Penn mean by the words next to the picture?

   _____

   _____

   _____

3. **a.** What did William Penn name the colony that he founded?

   _____

   b. What was the settlement's name?

   _____

4. Why did William Penn establish a colony?

   _____

   _____

   _____

5. List the three other Middle Colonies.

   _____

   _____

   _____

6. The people who settled the Middle Colonies brought a wide variety of skills and trades. How did this help the region?

   _____

   _____

   _____

McGraw-Hill School Division

USING ELEVATION AND RELIEF MAPS

Use the maps to answer the questions below. Underline your answers.
For help, you can refer to pages 214–215 in your textbook.

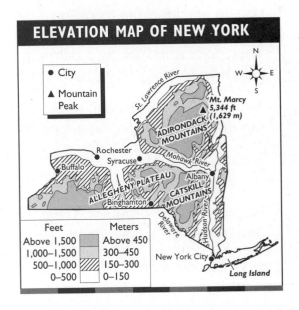

1. Which map shows you how elevation changes from place to place?

    a. the relief map

    b. the elevation map

2. Which map shows you how high the land is?

    a. the relief map

    b. the elevation map

3. In general what kind of relief does the northeastern part of New York have?

    a. low relief

    b. high relief

4. Why are the Adirondack Mountains shaded?

    a. they have low relief

    b. they have high relief

5. If you were to travel from Albany to Binghamton, what type of land would you see?

    a. flat plains

    b. hills and mountains

6. How tall is Mt. Marcy?

    a. under 2,500 ft.

    b. above 5,500 ft.

    c. above 5,000 ft.

    d. above 25,000 ft.

THE SOUTHERN COLONIES

Use the map to complete the activities on this page. For help, you can refer to pages 216–219 in your textbook.

1. Locate and label the following Southern Colonies on the map. Then color each colony a different color.

   Maryland—Red   Carolina—Blue
   Georgia—Green Virginia—Yellow

2. Locate and label the following settlements on the map:

   Baltimore   Charles Town
   Jamestown   Savannah

3. a. Which Southern Colony was later divided into two colonies?

   _____

   b. What were they called?

   _____

   _____

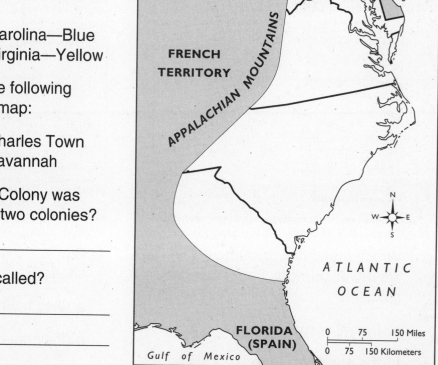

4. Why was Maryland founded?

   _____

   _____

5. What was good about Georgia's location?

   _____

   _____

6. Why did colonists pretend to "rent" enslaved Africans from South Carolina?

   _____

7. How was the geography of the Southern Colonies helpful to the colonists living there?

   _____

McGraw-Hill School Division

USING NEW WORDS

Choose a word from the box to complete each sentence. For help, you can refer to the lessons in Chapter 8 of your textbook.

Conestoga	proprietor	tolerate
covenant	indigo	debtor

1. If you were a person who owned land in a colony, you would be a

   _____.

2. If you allow people to have beliefs that are different from your own,

   you _____ the differences.

3. If you were talking about a plant that produces a blue dye, you might

   be referring to _____.

4. A large covered wagon built by the Pennsylvania Dutch is called a

   _____ wagon.

5. If you owed money to another person, you would be called a

   _____.

6. If you were talking about a special promise or agreement, you might

   be referring to a _____.

COMING TO THE ENGLISH COLONIES

Use the quotations on the right to complete the activities below. For help, you can refer to pages 224–227 in your textbook.

1. **a.** This man came from Scotland to settle in the English Colonies. Why do you think he left Scotland?

_____

b. List three things that the new colonies had to offer him.

_____

_____

_____

You would do well to advise all poor people . . . to take courage and come to this country.

2. **a.** This woman came to the colonies as an indentured servant. Why did some people choose to become indentured?

_____

_____

b. For how long was she going to be a servant?

_____

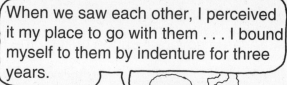

When we saw each other, I perceived it my place to go with them . . . I bound myself to them by indenture for three years.

3. **a.** Why was this man from Africa being brought to the English Colonies?

_____

b. What was he describing?

_____

_____

We were packed together in chains so tightly we could hardly move or turn over. . . . Many slaves fell sick and died.

McGraw-Hill School Division

LOOKING AT THE COLONIAL ECONOMY

Use the maps to complete the activities on this page. For help, you can refer to pages 228–233 in your textbook.

1. **a.** Draw a line to the map of the Southern Colonies.

    b. Why was this region well suited for growing crops?

    _____

    _____

    c. Name three cash crops grown in this region for export.

    _____

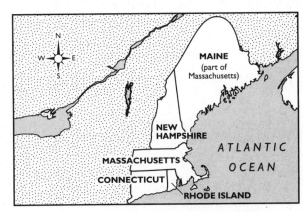

2. **a.** Draw a line to the map of the Middle Colonies.

    b. Why was this region called the "breadbasket of the colonies"?

    _____

    _____

    c. Where did the farmers in this region sell their surplus grain?

    _____

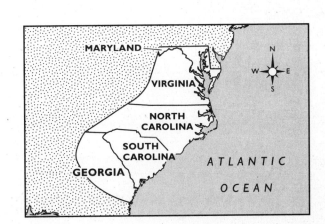

3. **a.** Draw a line to the map of the New England colonies.

    b. Name two ways New Englanders made a living.

    _____

    c. List four places where New Englanders sold their products.

    _____

    _____

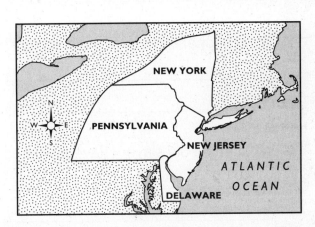

THINKING ABOUT COLONIAL SLAVERY

The picture below shows an advertisement that appeared in a newspaper in the 1700s. Use the ad to answer the questions. For help, you can refer to pages 236–241 in your textbook.

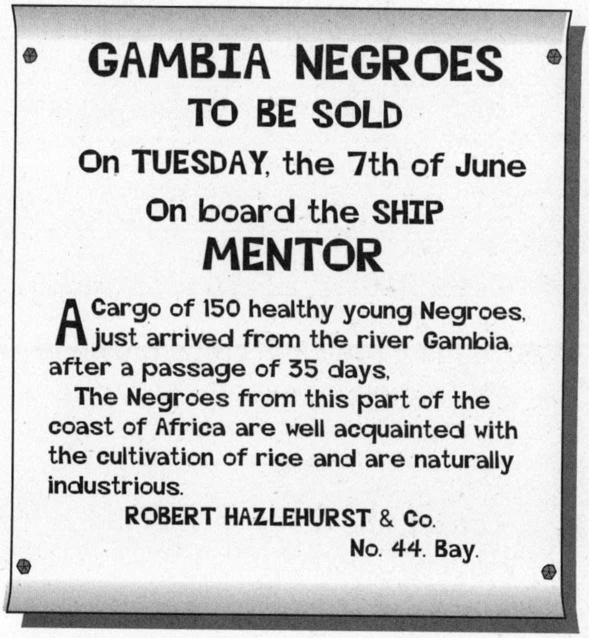

1. What is this advertisement for?

   _____

2. According to the ad, where were these Africans from?

   _____

   From which two present-day countries did most enslaved Africans come?

   _____

3. In which region of the English colonies would you expect to see this ad? Why?

GAMBIA NEGROES
TO BE SOLD
On TUESDAY, the 7th of June
On board the SHIP
MENTOR

A Cargo of 150 healthy young Negroes, just arrived from the river Gambia, after a passage of 35 days.
   The Negroes from this part of the coast of Africa are well acquainted with the cultivation of rice and are naturally industrious.
ROBERT HAZLEHURST & Co.
No. 44. Bay.

   _____

   _____

   _____

4. Why were there so many enslaved workers in this region?

   _____

   _____

5. What happened to families in slavery?

   _____

   _____

6. What effect did slavery have on the colonies?

   _____

   _____

   _____

McGraw-Hill School Division

USING CLIMOGRAPHS

Use the climographs below to answer the questions. For help, you can refer to pages 242–243 in your textbook.

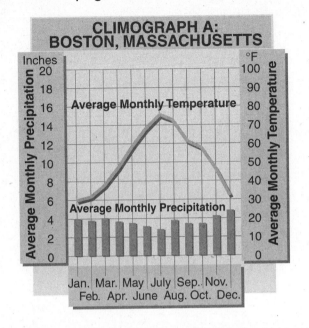

CLIMOGRAPH A:
BOSTON, MASSACHUSETTS

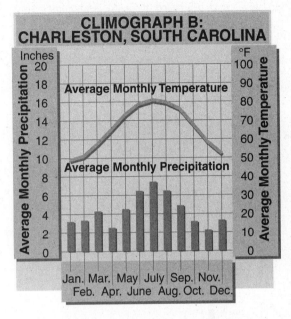

CLIMOGRAPH B:
CHARLESTON, SOUTH CAROLINA

1. What do climographs like the ones above show? _____

_____

2. Why are climographs useful? _____

3. What is Boston's average temperature in May? _____

   What is Charleston's average temperature in May? _____

4. In which city would you expect to have a rainy summer? Why? _____

_____

5. In which city would you expect to have a snowy winter? Why?

_____

6. When might you find a climograph like those above helpful?

_____

_____

_____

INTERVIEWING BENJAMIN FRANKLIN

Suppose you could interview Benjamin Franklin. Below are some
questions you might ask. In the spaces provided, write the answers you
think Franklin might give. For help, you can refer to pages 244–250 in
your textbook.

Interviewer: What was Philadelphia like when you moved there in 1723?

Franklin: _____

Interviewer: How did Philadelphia change during your lifetime?

Franklin: _____

_____

Interviewer: What were some of the many contributions you made to the city?

Franklin: _____

_____

_____

_____

Interviewer: How did you help African Americans?

Franklin: _____

Interviewer: How did your wife, Deborah Franklin, help with all the things you had
to do?

Franklin: _____

_____

Interviewer: Why do you think many colonists began moving to the backcountry in
the middle of the 1700s?

Franklin: _____

_____

Interviewer: What do you think are the keys to success?

Franklin: _____

McGraw-Hill School Division

WORKING WITH NEW WORDS

Write the letter of each word or term next to its meaning. For help, you can refer to the lessons in Chapter 9 of your textbook.

a. autobiography	**e.** export	**i.** slave trade	**m.** plantation
b. Middle Passage	**f.** frontier	**j.** agriculture	**n.** industry
c. free enterprise	**g.** almanac	**k.** backcountry	**o.** overseer
d. triangular trade	**h.** import	**l.** slave codes	

_____ 1. a large Southern farm that grew only one crop

_____ 2. the name colonists gave to the rugged land near the Appalachian Mountains

_____ 3. a system in which people can start a business, deciding what to make, how much to produce, and what price to charge

_____ 4. the business of buying and selling people for profit

_____ 5. the triangular trade route's middle leg, which began in Africa and ended in the West Indies

_____ 6. the business of farming

_____ 7. the boss of a plantation

_____ 8. a reference book providing facts about stars and weather

_____ 9. the story of a person's own life, written by himself or herself

_____ 10. to send goods to other countries for sale or trade

_____ 11. a trade route whose legs formed a triangle from the colonies, to Africa, then to the West Indies, and back to the colonies

_____ 12. to bring in goods from another country for sale or use

_____ 13. all the businesses that make one kind of product or provide one kind of service

_____ 14. rules used to keep enslaved workers under control

_____ 15. a word used by colonists to describe land on the edge of a European settlement

NEW SPAIN AND THE SPANISH MISSIONS

Use the map to complete the activities below. For help, you can refer to pages 256–261 in your textbook.

1. Label these four areas of New Spain on the map:

    Mexico   New Mexico
    California   Texas

2. Draw the route of El Camino Real on the map in red.

Which parts of New Spain did El Camino Real connect?

_____

_____

3. Put an X on the city where "the Alamo Chain" was located.

What does "the Alamo Chain" refer to?

_____

_____

4. Locate and label the first Spanish mission in California.

_____

5. What was the purpose of the missions?

_____

_____

_____

6. Why did the Pueblo revolt against the Spanish?

_____

_____

_____

_____

THE BUILDERS OF NEW FRANCE

Read the paragraphs below. Fill in the blanks to complete the activity. For help, you can refer to pages 264–269 in your textbook.

In the 1600s France wanted to start a colony in North America to help its

_____. The French were also still looking for the

_____ to Asia.

In 1608 Samuel de Champlain founded _____, the

first permanent French settlement. He made friends with a Native American group,

_____, by learning to speak their language and

_____.

In 1673 _____ and _____

set out on the Mississippi River in search of the Northwest Passage. They turned

back when they realized the river flowed _____, not west.

The first European to see the mouth of the Mississippi River was

_____. He claimed all of the _____ valley

for France. He named these lands _____.

MAKING CONCLUSIONS

Use the pictures and words on the right to complete the activities on this page. For help, you can refer to pages 270–271 in your textbook.

1. This picture shows Samuel de Champlain with a Huron. Read Champlain's words. Then put an X next to the conclusion you think he made about the Huron.

They speak very deliberately [carefully], and reflect [think] for a good while. I assure you that plenty of them have good judgment.

_____ The Huron are a reckless people.

_____ The Huron are a thoughtful and intelligent people.

_____ The Huron are likely to fight us over the fur trade.

2. This picture shows Robert La Salle. Read the words La Salle might have said. Then put an X next to the conclusion you can draw.

I hereby claim all the land of the Mississippi River valley for France and name these lands Louisiana in honor of my king, Louis XIV.

_____ La Salle honored the king of France.

_____ La Salle wanted the lands for himself.

_____ La Salle wanted all the glory for himself.

3. This picture shows a voyageur at a French trading post. Read what he says about his life. Then put an X next to the conclusion you can draw.

There is no life so happy as a voyageur's life; none so independent; no place where a man enjoys so much variety and freedom.

_____ He has had many bad experiences.

_____ He was forced into trading his furs with the French.

_____ He greatly enjoys his life.

THE CHANGING FACE OF NORTH AMERICA

Use the maps below to answer the questions on this page. For help, you can refer to pages 272–275 in your textbook

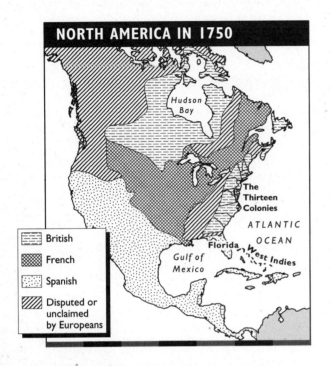

1. Which three nations are represented on the maps above?

_____

_____

2. Which war took place between the dates on the two maps?

_____

3. Which two nations fought against each other during this war?

_____

4. What caused the war?

_____

_____

_____

5. Which countries gained land between 1750 and 1763?

_____

6. Which country lost land between 1750 and 1763?

_____

7. As a result of this war, which regions of North America did Britain gain control over?

_____

_____

_____

McGraw-Hill School Division

LINKING NEW WORDS AND IDEAS

Write a term from the box next to the sentence or sentences that tell about it. For help, you can refer to the lessons in Chapter 10 of your textbook.

mission	voyageur	Treaty of Paris	French and Indian War
portage	coureur de bois	Proclamation of 1763	

_____ 1. This is what the British called the fighting between the British colonists and the French and their Native American allies.

_____ 2. This document, signed by Great Britain and France in 1763, officially ended the French and Indian War.

_____ 3. This document, issued by King George III of Great Britain, gave all the land east of the Appalachian Mountains to the British colonists. It set aside lands west of the mountains for Native Americans.

_____ 4. This was a settlement where missionaries lived, worked, and tried to convert Native Americans to Christianity.

_____ 5. This term was used to describe a person who trapped furs without permission from the French government.

_____ 6. This word refers to a land route from one body of water to another.

_____ 7. This was a person in New France who transported furs and other goods by canoe to Quebec.

McGraw-Hill School Division

GOVERNING COLONIAL AMERICA

Write each item from the box under the picture it goes with. Then answer the questions. For help, you can refer to pages 286–291 in your textbook.

> - chosen by English King
> - delegates are usually white, Protestant, male landowners
> - have the power to dissolve the colonial assemblies
> - make laws for the colonies and call for taxes
> - raise money for the militia
> - enforce English laws in the colonies

Royal governors

Colonial assemblies

1. _____

_____

2. _____

_____

3. _____

_____

4. _____

_____

5. _____

_____

6. _____

_____

7. What did the colonial delegates speak up for in their assemblies?

_____

8. What important right did John Peter Zenger's trial establish in the colonies?

_____

THE GROWING CONFLICT

Use the sentences in the box to make a chart that shows how the conflict grew between the British and the colonists. Then answer the questions that follow. The first event has been filled in for you. For help, you can refer to pages 292–297 in your textbook.

- With the Intolerable Acts, Britain closes Boston Harbor and orders the colonists to shelter British soldiers.

- The Townshend Acts make the colonists pay taxes on everyday products imported from Britain.

- British soldiers kill five colonists during the Boston Massacre.

- The British Parliament passes the Stamp Act to collect taxes from the colonies.

- The colonies form Committees of Correspondence to keep each other informed about important events.

- The Boston Tea Party takes place to protest the British tax on tea.

DATE	EVENT
1765	The British Parliament passes the Stamp Act to collect taxes from the colonies.
1767	
1770	
1772	
1773	
1774	

Which event was the most important in uniting the colonists? Why?

_____

_____

McGraw-Hill School Division

READING POLITICAL CARTOONS

Use the political cartoon to help you complete the activities on this page.
For help, you can refer to pages 298–299 in your textbook.

Take back your trash!

1. What is a political cartoon? _____

_____

_____

2. What is the political cartoon above about?

_____

_____

3. Whom does the image of the king symbolize?

_____

How do you know? _____

_____

4. What do the bags of trash symbolize? _____

How do you know? _____

5. Whom do the people throwing the bags of trash stand for? _____

How do you know? _____

_____

THE AMERICAN REVOLUTION BEGINS

Use the map to complete the activities on this page. For help, you can refer to pages 300–305 in your textbook.

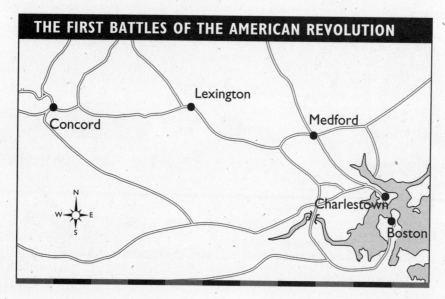

1. Find the route Paul Revere took on April 18, 1775. Trace it in blue.

   Why did Revere make this ride?

   _____

   _____

   _____

2. Find the location of the first battle of the American Revolution. Circle it in green.

   What was another name for men in the colonial militia?

   _____

3. Trace in red the route the British took after the first battle.

   What were the British planning to do in the next town?

   _____

   What was the outcome of this battle?

   _____

   _____

4. Which other military events proved that the colonists were serious in their struggle against Britain?

   _____

   _____

5. What did colonial unity and military readiness in these early battles lay the groundwork for?

   _____

   _____

   _____

MATCHING WORDS AND THEIR MEANINGS

Write the letter of the term that matches each definition. For help, you can refer to the lessons in Chapter 11 of your textbook.

a. militia	**f.** First Continental Congress	**k.** Townshend Acts	**p.** Stamp Act
b. rebel	**g.** American Revolution	**l.** Intolerable Acts	**q.** minutemen
c. repeal	**h.** Battle of Bunker Hill	**m.** Sons of Liberty	**r.** assembly
d. liberty	**i.** Boston Tea Party	**n.** town meeting	**s.** delegate
e. boycott	**j.** Committees of Correspondence	**o.** treason	**t.** petition

_____ 1. a lawmaking body

_____ 2. citizens who gather to solve local problems

_____ 3. a volunteer military force

_____ 4. a member of an assembly

_____ 5. freedom

_____ 6. to refuse to obey those in charge because of different ideas about what is right

_____ 7. one of the first British laws taxing the colonies

_____ 8. the betrayal of one's country by helping an enemy

_____ 9. groups of colonists who organized protests against the British government

_____ 10. to cancel or take back

_____ 11. laws that made colonists pay taxes on everyday items imported from Britain

_____ 12. to refuse to do business or have contact with a person, group, or country

_____ 13. committees formed by the colonies to keep each other informed

_____ 14. a protest in which colonists dumped chests of tea into Boston Harbor

_____ 15. the reaction of the British Parliament to the Boston Tea Party

_____ 16. a meeting of colonial delegates to decide on a plan to oppose the Intolerable Acts

_____ 17. trained soldiers, ready at a minute's notice

_____ 18. the war between the colonists and the British

_____ 19. a famous battle between the British and minutemen

_____ 20. a written request signed by many people

THE DECLARATION OF INDEPENDENCE

Thomas Jefferson, the author of the Declaration of Independence, called it "an expression of the American mind." Read this excerpt from the Declaration. Then answer the questions that follow. For help, refer to pages 310–317 in your textbook.

We hold these truths to be self-evident that all men are created equal, that they are endowed by their Creator with certain unalienable rights, that among these are life, liberty, and the pursuit of happiness. That to secure these rights, governments are instituted among men, deriving their just powers from the consent of the governed, that whenever any form of government becomes destructive of these ends, it is the right of the people to alter or to abolish it, and to institute new government, laying its foundation on such principles and organizing its powers in such form, as to them shall seem most likely to effect their safety and happiness.

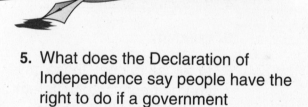

1. What was the purpose of the Declaration of Independence?

_____

_____

2. On what date was the Declaration of Independence approved?

_____

3. What is the first truth mentioned in the Declaration of Independence?

_____

4. What unalienable rights does the Declaration say people have?

_____

_____

5. What does the Declaration of Independence say people have the right to do if a government becomes destructive?

_____

_____

_____

6. Why is the Declaration of Independence one of the most important documents in history?

_____

_____

_____

_____

McGraw-Hill School Division

TURNING POINTS IN THE AMERICAN REVOLUTION

The map shows three major battles. Use the map to do the activities below. Refer to pages 320–325 in your textbook.

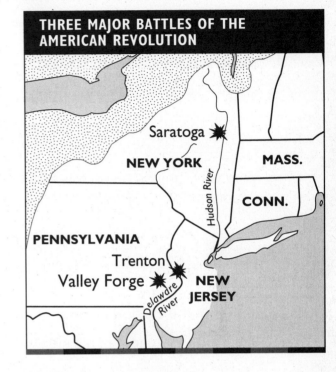

1. Circle Trenton in red on the map.

How was the battle won?

_____

_____

_____

_____

2. Circle Saratoga in green.

Why was the battle at Saratoga a turning point in the war?

_____

_____

3. Circle Valley Forge in blue.

What happened to the American troops during their winter there?

_____

4. Who led the Continental Army during all three of these battles?

_____

What kind of military experience did he have? _____

_____

_____

5. What were the Continental Army's weaknesses? _____

_____

6. What were its strengths? _____

_____

_____

HELPING WIN THE REVOLUTION

Use the pictures below to complete the activities on this page. For help, you can refer to pages 328–335 in your textbook.

1. a. Draw a line to the picture of the person who led American troops in the West.

    b. What was the name of the fort he captured from the British?

_____

    c. Why was the capture of this fort important for the Americans?

_____

_____

John Paul Jones

2. a. Draw a line to the picture of the leader of the Patriots at sea.

    b. What was the name of his ship?

_____

    c. What did his victory prove about the American troops?

_____

_____

George Rogers Clark

3. a. Draw a line to the picture of the person who helped American soldiers on the battlefield.

    b. How did she help?

_____

_____

_____

    c. What was her nickname?

_____

Mary Ludwig Hays

COMPARING MAPS AT DIFFERENT SCALES

Use the maps below to complete the activities on this page. For help, you can refer to pages 336–337 in your textbook.

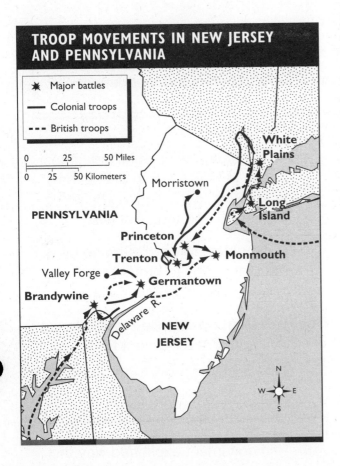

1. How many colonies are shown on the small-scale map? _____

   How many colonies are shown on the large-scale map? _____

2. Which would you use to find the route that colonial troops used through New

   Jersey? _____

3. What does the large-scale map show that the small-scale map does not?

   _____

4. Suppose you were Washington planning the battles in the Middle Colonies. Which map would be more helpful? Why?

   _____

LINKING NEW WORDS AND IDEAS

Write each term from the box next to the sentence that tells something about it. For help, you can refer to the lessons in Chapter 12 of your textbook.

traitor	mercenary	Treaty of Paris	Second Continental Congress
Patriot	Loyalist	Continental Army	Declaration of Independence

_____ **1.** This meeting of colonial delegates began in May 1775 to decide how to respond to the fighting between the British and the colonists.

_____ **2.** This fighting force was made up of colonial troops to protect the colonies against British attack.

_____ **3.** This term was applied to a colonist who supported the fight for independence.

_____ **4.** This term describes someone who turns against his or her country.

_____ **5.** This document explained why the colonies were breaking away from Great Britain and set out the rights and responsibilities of people in a democracy.

_____ **6.** This is a soldier who is paid to fight for another country.

_____ **7.** This term was applied to a colonist who remained loyal to Britain during the American Revolution.

_____ **8.** In this 1783 document the British recognized the United States' independence and agreed upon new boundaries for the United States.

McGraw-Hill School Division

FACTS ABOUT THE ARTICLES OF CONFEDERATION

Read each of the following statements. If it is true, write **True** after it. If a statement is false, write **False** after it. Then write the reasons for your answer in the space provided. For help, refer to pages 342–345 in your textbook.

1. The cartoon at the right shows one of the major weaknesses of the Articles of Confederation.

   _____

   _____

   _____

   _____

2. The Articles of Confederation gave almost all power to the central government.

   _____

   _____

3. The Articles of Confederation led to conflicts between the states about money.

   _____

   _____

4. The Articles of Confederation made it easy for Congress to resolve conflicts

   between the states. _____

   _____

5. Shays's Rebellion had little effect on how people felt about the Articles and the

   new government. _____

   _____

6. The Northwest Ordinance was an important law passed by Congress under the

   Articles. _____

   _____

   _____

PLANNING A NEW GOVERNMENT

Think about what happened at the Constitutional Convention. Then complete the activities on this page. For help, you can refer to pages 346–351 in your textbook.

1. Explain how the framers of the Virginia Plan and the New Jersey Plan proposed to decide on the number of representatives in Congress.

   Virginia Plan: _____

   _____

   New Jersey Plan: _____

   _____

2. What compromise did the states finally reach?

   _____

   _____

   _____

   _____

3. What was the compromise called? _____

4. Describe another compromise the Convention's delegates reached.

   _____

   _____

5. Complete the chart below to show how the delegates agreed to organize the national government.

BRANCH OF GOVERNMENT	RESPONSIBILITY
Legislative	
Executive	
Judicial	

McGraw-Hill School Division

RECOGNIZING POINT OF VIEW

Read the statement each person made about the new Constitution. Then read each question below and circle the letter next to the correct answer. For help, you can refer to pages 352–353 in your textbook.

> My political curiosity . . . leads me to ask: Who authorized them to speak the language of *We the people*, instead of, *We the states*? . . . The federal Convention ought [only] to have amended the old system; for this purpose they were solely delegated.

> Sir, I agree with this Constitution with all its faults, if they are such; because I think a general government necessary for us. . . . I doubt too whether any other Convention we can obtain may be able to make a better Constitution.

Patrick Henry

Benjamin Franklin

1. What was Patrick Henry's point of view?

   a. He felt that the delegates to the Constitutional Convention should have amended the old form of government.

   b. He felt that the delegates had done a good job writing the Constitution and establishing a new form of government.

   c. He felt that an entirely new Constitution should have been written.

2. What was Benjamin Franklin's point of view?

   a. He felt that a new Convention should be assembled to try to write another Constitution.

   b. He supported the Constitution even if it wasn't perfect because he felt it was the best one that had been written.

   c. He felt that the new Constitution had many faults and didn't deserve to be supported by him or anyone else.

3. What is a person's point of view?_____

_____

_____

McGraw-Hill School Division

THINKING ABOUT THE CONSTITUTION

Read the chart. Then complete each item below. For help, you can refer to pages 354–357 in your textbook.

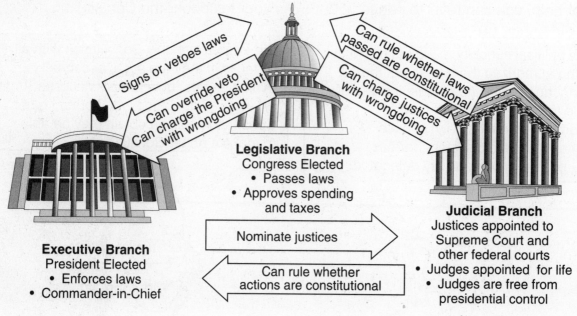

Executive Branch
President Elected
• Enforces laws
• Commander-in-Chief

Legislative Branch
Congress Elected
• Passes laws
• Approves spending and taxes

Signs or vetoes laws

Can override veto
Can charge the President with wrongdoing

Can rule whether laws passed are constitutional

Can charge justices with wrongdoing

Nominate justices

Can rule whether actions are constitutional

Judicial Branch
Justices appointed to Supreme Court and other federal courts
• Judges appointed for life
• Judges are free from presidential control

1. Why did the authors of the Constitution set up the system of checks and

   balances? _____

   _____

2. How does this system affect the branches of government? _____

   _____

   _____

3. Study the chart and review Lesson 3 in your textbook. Then circle the letter next to each sentence that gives an example of how the system works.

   a. The President can order the army into battle; only Congress can declare war.

   b. Congress has the power to appoint the President.

   c. The President can veto laws passed by Congress.

   d. The Supreme Court can stop a law passed by Congress if the law does not follow the Constitution.

4. What system of government did the Constitution set up? _____

   How does this system share power? _____

   _____

THINKING ABOUT THE NEW GOVERNMENT

Complete the activities on this page. Refer to pages 358–363 in your textbook.

1. The Federalists and the Antifederalists disagreed about the Constitution. Use the chart below to explain each side's point of view.

FEDERALISTS	ANTIFEDERALISTS

2. a. What role did James Madison, Alexander Hamilton, and John Jay play in persuading reluctant states to ratify the Constitution?

_____

b. What role did John Hancock play? _____

_____

3. What amendments did Congress make in the Constitution to fulfill John

Hancock's promise? _____

4. To help the President run the government, Congress set up a Cabinet. Each Cabinet member headed an office or department. Complete the chart below by describing the responsibilities of each office or department.

DEPARTMENT OR OFFICE	RESPONSIBILITY
Treasury	
State	
War	
Attorney General	

MATCHING TERMS WITH THEIR MEANINGS

Write the letter of the term from the box that matches each definition. For help, you can refer to the lessons in Chapter 13 of your textbook.

a. veto	**f.** Constitutional Convention	**k.** executive branch	**p.** judicial branch
b. Senate	**g.** House of Representatives	**l.** Antifederalists	**q.** political party
c. preamble	**h.** Articles of Confederation	**m.** Supreme Court	**r.** amendment
d. Cabinet	**i.** legislative branch	**n.** Great Compromise	**s.** federal system
e. Federalists	**j.** New Jersey Plan	**o.** checks and balances	**t.** Bill of Rights

_____ 1. the document that set up our country's first central government

_____ 2. the meeting at which delegates wrote the Constitution

_____ 3. the lawmaking branch of government

_____ 4. the branch of government that carries out the laws made by Congress

_____ 5. the branch of government that decides the meaning of the laws

_____ 6. the head of the judicial branch of government

_____ 7. it gave small and large states an equal number of representatives

_____ 8. a proposal that Congress should have two separate houses

_____ 9. the house of Congress in which representation is based on population

_____ 10. the house of Congress in which each state has two representatives

_____ 11. an addition to a constitution or other document

_____ 12. an introduction to a document

_____ 13. a system in which the states and the federal government share power

_____ 14. a system in which one branch of government is balanced by another

_____ 15. to refuse to approve

_____ 16. supporters of the ratification of the Constitution

_____ 17. opponents of the ratification of the Constitution

_____ 18. the ten amendments that were added to the Constitution

_____ 19. government departments set up to help the President

_____ 20. a group of people who share similar ideas about government

THINKING ABOUT THE WAY WEST

Use the map to help you complete the activities on this page. For help, you can refer to pages 374–377 in your textbook.

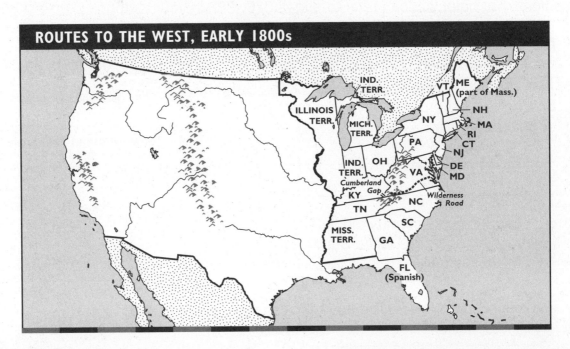

ROUTES TO THE WEST, EARLY 1800s

1. Label the Appalachian Mountains on the map.

Why didn't pioneers settle there?

_____

_____

2. Label the Mississippi River. Trace its route in blue.

3. Label the Central Plains and the Gulf Coastal Plain.

Why did the pioneers leave the East to settle on these plains?

_____

_____

_____

4. What did trailblazers do to help the pioneers reach the West? What trails did they often use?

_____

_____

_____

5. Find the Cumberland Gap. What famous trailblazer crossed the gap to settle in Kentucky?

_____

6. Why was the Wilderness Road important?

_____

_____

_____

HEADLINES DURING THE TIME OF JEFFERSON

Below are headlines that might have appeared in United States newspapers in the early 1800s. Read each headline and answer the questions. For help, you can refer to pages 378–383 in your textbook.

1. a. When would this headline have appeared?

_____

b. What did Jefferson believe was the best government?

_____

_____

c. What European country did Jefferson believe was a threat to the United States?

_____

_____

Jefferson Becomes President

Today, Thomas Jefferson began his duties as President of the United States.

2. a. When would this headline have appeared?

_____

b. What was this land and deal called?

_____

c. What lands did the United States acquire with this deal?

_____

_____

_____

U.S. and France Make Land Deal

President Jefferson announced today that the United States had reached an agreement with France.

3. a. When would this headline have appeared?

_____

b. What was Lewis and Clark's goal?

_____

_____

c. What Native American helped them?

_____

Lewis and Clark Reach Goal

Eighteen months after they set out to explore the Louisiana Territory, Lewis and Clark finally reached their goal.

McGraw-Hill School Division

EVENTS IN THE WAR OF 1812

The excerpt below is from a letter written by Isaac Hull, captain of the *Constitution,* after his sea battle with a British ship, the *Guerrière.* Read the excerpt, and then answer the questions. For help, you can refer to pages 386–391 in your textbook.

After informing you that so fine a ship as the *Guerrière* . . . had been totally . . . cut to pieces so as to make her not worth towing into port . . . you can have no doubt of the gallantry and good conduct of the officers and ship's company I have the honor to command. It only remains . . . to assure you that they all fought with great bravery.

—Isaac Hull

Richard Morris and James Woodress, editors, *Voices from America's Past* (New York: E. P. Dutton, 1963).

1. Whose warship was the *Guerrière*?

_____

2. What happened to the *Guerrière*?

_____

_____

3. What war was taking place when the letter was written?

_____

4. Who was at war?

_____

_____

5. What was the cause of the war?

_____

_____

_____

6. Why was the war more difficult on land than at sea for the Americans?

_____

_____

7. What did African Americans gain?

_____

_____

_____

8. How did war benefit the United States?

_____

_____

_____

_____

COMPARING MAPS

Use the maps below to help you complete the activities on this page. For help, you can refer to pages 392–393 in your textbook.

MAP A: BATTLES OF THE WAR OF 1812

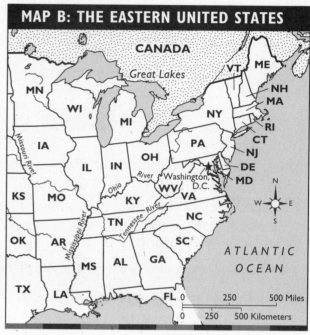

MAP B: THE EASTERN UNITED STATES

1. What kind of map is Map A?

   political   relief   historical

2. What kind of map is Map B?

   political   relief   historical

3. In which present-day state did the battle of Horseshoe Bend take place?

   _____

   How did you find the answer?

   _____

   _____

   _____

4. Locate the state of Wisconsin on Map B. What was this area called during the War of 1812?

   _____

   How did you find the answer?

   _____

   _____

5. Which two of the maps listed below would you use if you wanted to find out if any battles during the War of 1812 were fought in mountainous areas?

   political   relief   historical

McGraw-Hill School Division

ANDREW JACKSON'S PRESIDENCY

The poster below could have been made when Jackson ran for President. Use the poster to answer the questions below. For help, you can refer to pages 394–399 in your textbook.

1. The poster refers to Jackson as "Old Hickory." Why was he given this nickname?

    _____

    _____

    _____

2. Why does the poster refer to Jackson as a "People's President"?

    _____

    _____

    _____

    _____

3. What changes in the voting laws may have helped Jackson win the election?

    _____

    _____

    _____

4. What kind of government did Jackson believe in? _____

    _____

5. What was one of the most difficult issues President Jackson faced?

    _____

    _____

6. How did Jackson want to solve this issue? _____

    _____

7. What did the government do to solve this issue? _____

    _____

    _____

THINKING ABOUT NEW WORDS

Write each word or term from the box under the phrase that tells about it.
For help, you can refer to the lessons in Chapter 14 of your textbook.

pioneer	Louisiana Purchase	national anthem
neutral	Era of Good Feelings	Trail of Tears
War Hawks	Indian Removal Act	War of 1812
	Battle of New Orleans	

1. the 800-mile journey United States soldiers forced the Cherokee to take from Georgia to Indian Territory

   _____

2. a person who leads the way into new areas

   _____

3. a law that allowed the President to remove Native Americans from their homelands

   _____

4. the land west of the Mississippi River that the United States purchased from France in 1803

   _____

5. a period of peace and prosperity for the United States that began at the end of the War of 1812

   _____

6. not taking sides on an issue

   _____

7. an 1815 battle led by Andrew Jackson against the British that led to a great victory for the United States

   _____

8. members of Congress during Madison's Presidency who wanted to declare war against Great Britain

   _____

9. a song such as "The Star-Spangled Banner" that praises a country

   _____

10. a conflict between Great Britain and the United States that began because Great Britain started taking American ships and sailors

    _____

McGraw-Hill School Division

MACHINES OF THE INDUSTRIAL REVOLUTION

Use the pictures below to complete the activities. In the space provided
identify each machine, the person who developed it, and the effect it had.
For help, you can refer to pages 404–409 in your textbook.

Machine: _____

Developed by: _____

Effect: _____

_____

_____

Machine: _____

Developed by: _____

Effect: _____

_____

_____

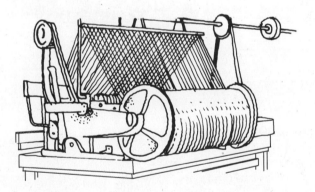

Machine: _____

Developed by: _____

Effect: _____

_____

_____

_____

Machine: _____

Developed by: _____

Effect: _____

_____

_____

_____

DEVELOPMENTS IN TRANSPORTATION

Use the pictures to help you complete the activities on this page. For help, you can refer to pages 410–414 in your textbook.

1. a. Draw a line to the picture that shows how Robert Fulton helped improve transportation.

   b. What made Fulton's idea possible?

   _____

   c. What did Fulton's idea prove? _____

   _____

   _____

Tom Thumb

2. a. Draw a line to the picture that shows how DeWitt Clinton helped improve transportation.

   b. What two bodies of water did this human-made waterway connect?

   _____

   c. How did the waterway affect trade in the

   United States? _____

   _____

   _____

Clermont

3. a. Draw a line to the picture that shows how Peter Cooper helped improve transportation.

   b. What did Peter Cooper's idea replace?

   _____

   c. What did Cooper's idea prove? _____

   _____

   _____

Erie Canal

McGraw-Hill School Division

A CHART OF TEXAS HISTORY

Use the information in the box to complete the chart of Texas history. Then answer the questions below. The first event has been filled in for you. For help, you can refer to pages 416–421 in your textbook.

> - Stephen Austin leads 300 American families to settle in Texas.
> - Mexican soldiers defeat the Texas Army at The Alamo.
> - The Mexican government jails Stephen Austin.
> - Mexican leaders stop all immigration from the United States.
> - Texas becomes the 28th state of the United States.
> - Mexico, which includes Texas, wins independence from Spain.
> - Santa Anna grants Texas its independence.

DATE	EVENT
1821	Mexico, which includes Texas, wins independence from Spain.
1822	
1830	
1833	
March 1836	
April 1836	
1845	

1. For how many years was Texas a part of Mexico? _____

2. How many years was it from the time Mexico became independent from Spain until Texas became the 28th state? _____

3. Why was Texas statehood delayed all those years? _____

_____

_____

THE MEXICAN WAR

The excerpt below is from the diary of President James K. Polk. He wrote these words in May 1846. Read the excerpt. Then answer the questions that follow. For help, you can refer to pages 422–425 in your textbook.

At seven o'clock P.M. my private secretary returned from the Capitol and announced to me that the bill which passed the House of Representatives . . . yesterday, making a formal declaration of war against Mexico, had passed the Senate by a vote of 42 ayes and 2 noes. . . . He [reported] to me that the debate in the Senate today was most animating and thrilling.

—James K. Polk

Allan Nevins, *Polk: Diary of a President* (New York: Putnam Publishing Group, 1968).

1. Which war does President Polk refer to in the entry?

   _____

2. What bill does Polk say was passed by the Senate?

   _____

   _____

   How many Senators voted for the bill, and how many voted against it?

   _____

3. What event caused this war?

   _____

   _____

   _____

4. About how long did the war last?

   _____

5. What battle ended the war?

   _____

6. How much of its territory was Mexico forced to give up to the United States?

   _____

7. How did the borders of the United States change after the war?

   _____

   _____

   _____

McGraw-Hill School Division

USING REFERENCE SOURCES

Suppose you are writing a report about the Mexican War. Draw a line from the information you want to find to the picture that shows where to find it. Then give a reason for choosing that reference source. For help, you can refer to pages 426–427 in your textbook.

1. You want to find a map that shows key battles in the Mexican War.

Reason: _____

_____

2. You need to find information about General Winfield Scott.

Reason: _____

_____

_____

Which volume would you look in?

_____

_____

3. You need a book about Zachary Taylor, but don't have a title.

Reason: _____

_____

How would you find the book you want?

_____

_____

_____

4. You need some geographical information about Mexico.

Reason: _____

_____

_____

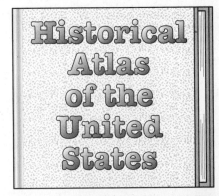

IDENTIFYING WESTERN TRAILS

Use the map to complete the activities that follow. For help, you can refer to pages 428–433 in your textbook.

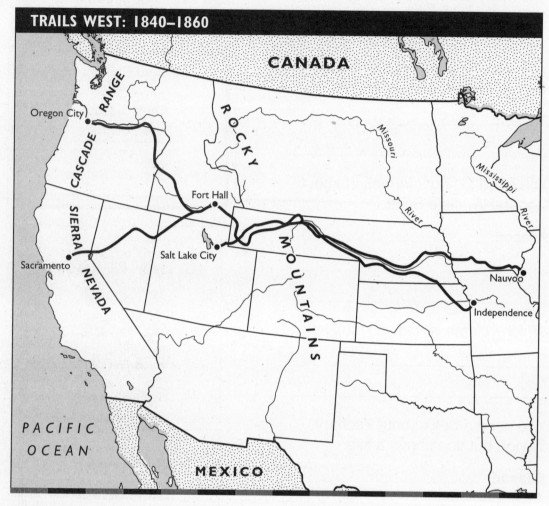

TRAILS WEST: 1840–1860

1. a. Label the Oregon Trail. Trace its route in green.

b. Why did large numbers of people travel west? _____

_____

2. a. Label the Mormon Trail. Trace its route in brown.

b. How did this trail get its name? _____

_____

3. a. Label the California Trail. Trace its route in red.
b. What event caused large numbers of people to travel across this trail?

_____

McGraw-Hill School Division

LINKING NEW WORDS AND IDEAS

Write each word or term from the box next to the sentence that tells something about it. For help, you can refer to Chapter 15 in your textbook.

steam engine	reaper	cotton gin	Treaty of Guadalupe Hidalgo
stagecoach	lock	investor	interchangeable parts
Forty-Niners	canal	gold rush	Industrial Revolution

_____ 1. a person who uses money to buy or make something that will make more money

_____ 2. a horse-drawn carriage used to carry passengers, baggage, and mail

_____ 3. During this event, large numbers of people went to California seeking gold.

_____ 4. standard-sized parts that are easily replaced

_____ 5. This machine was used to remove the seeds from cotton.

_____ 6. This kind of engine uses steam to create power.

_____ 7. During this period, goods that had been made by hand were now made by machines, often in factories.

_____ 8. This structure is a human-made waterway.

_____ 9. searched for gold in California in 1849

_____ 10. uses sharp blades to cut and harvest grain

_____ 11. ended the Mexican War

_____ 12. a kind of water elevator that moves boats to higher or lower levels

COMPARING THE NORTH AND THE SOUTH

The maps below show how the country was divided on slavery. Circle the name of the region that each sentence describes. For help, you can refer to pages 444–449 in your textbook.

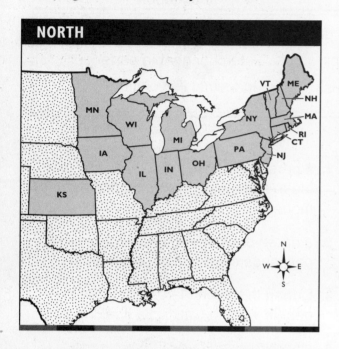

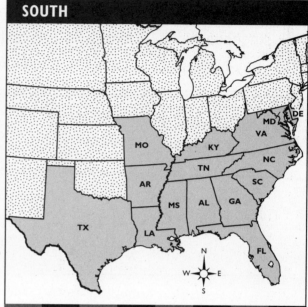

1. This region had become wealthy because of the cotton grown and produced by slave labor.

   North   South

2. Manufacturing was becoming much more important in this region's economy.

   North   South

3. Many immigrants from Ireland and Germany settled in this region.

   North   South

4. About four million enslaved African Americans were forced to work on the cotton plantations in this region.

   North   South

5. Most states in this region had ended slavery.

   North   South

6. Some states in this region made it a crime to teach a slave to read or write.

   North   South

7. A number of slave rebellions took place in this region.

   North   South

8. Even though most states in this region had ended slavery, there was much prejudice against African Americans.

   North   South

PEOPLE FIGHTING FOR EQUALITY

Use the pictures on the right to complete the activities. Write the number of each statement on the line next to the picture of the person or people it describes. For help, you can refer to pages 452–457 in your textbook.

1. This person started a newspaper called *The Liberator*. He believed that slavery was wrong and should be ended.

Lucretia Mott and Elizabeth Cady Stanton

2. These sisters, daughters of a plantation owner, were the first women to speak publicly for the abolitionist cause.

William Lloyd Garrison

3. More than 300 enslaved people owed their freedom to this former slave.

Sojourner Truth

4. These women organized the Seneca Falls Convention, the first convention to discuss the rights of women.

Harriet Tubman

5. This former enslaved person traveled the country giving speeches in support of abolition and women's rights.

Sarah and Angelina Grimké

McGraw-Hill School Division

READING A NEWSPAPER

The article below might have appeared in a newspaper in 1831. Read the article. Then complete the activities that follow. For help, you can refer to pages 458–459 in your textbook.

Garrison Publishes Abolitionist Newspaper

Boston, Massachusetts, January 2, 1831

In Boston yesterday Mr. William Lloyd Garrison began publication of his controversial newspaper, *The Liberator*. Its abolitionist message promises to enrage some and offer encouragement to others.

In a front-page editorial, Garrison argued for the immediate freedom of all slaves! He also promised that The Liberator would stir the conscience of the nation as never before.

Reaction in some parts of the South has been extreme. Many Southern leaders have demanded that Garrison be jailed. Some have even gone so far as to offer rewards for his kidnapping. Already jailed once for his abolitionist views, Garrison seems unaffected by these threats and remains steadfast in his commitment to the abolitionist cause.

1. Circle the headline. What is a headline meant to do?

   _____

   _____

2. Underline the dateline. What does a dateline tell you?

   _____

   _____

3. The article gives facts about a recent event. What kind of article is it?

   _____

4. What is the article about?

   _____

   _____

5. When and where did the event described in the article take place?

   _____

   _____

6. Where in the newspaper would you look to find the editor's opinion about the event or article?

   _____

   _____

CHARTING EVENTS LEADING TO WAR

Use the events in the box to complete the chart below. Then write a sentence next to each event that explains its effect or result. Some events and their effects have been filled in for you. For help, you can refer to pages 460–465 in your textbook.

> - The Confederate States of America was formed.
> - The Compromise of 1850 was approved.
> - Congress passed the Kansas-Nebraska Act.
> - John Brown raided Harpers Ferry.
> - The Supreme Court made the Dred Scott Decision.
> - Harriet Beecher Stowe wrote *Uncle Tom's Cabin.*
> - Lincoln was elected President.

EVENTS LEADING TO WAR		
DATE	EVENT	EFFECT OR RESULT
1850	The Compromise of 1850 was approved.	California was admitted as a free state. In return the North accepted the Fugitive Slave Law.
1852	Harriet Beecher Stowe wrote *Uncle Tom's Cabin.*	
1854		Kansas and Nebraska were allowed to decide for themselves whether to allow slavery.
1857	The Supreme Court made the Dred Scott Decision.	
1859		Southerners now feared that Northerners would stop at nothing to abolish slavery.
1860	Lincoln was elected President.	
1861		The Union was split apart.

USING NEW WORDS

Choose a term from the box to answer each definition. For help, you can refer to the lessons in Chapter 16 of your textbook.

secede	Compromise of 1850	Kansas-Nebraska Act
abolitionist	Dred Scott Decision	Seneca Falls Convention
states' rights	Fugitive Slave Law	Underground Railroad
Confederate States of America		Missouri Compromise

1. said enslaved people were property

   _____

2. used to refer to a state's leaving the Union

   _____

3. the name of the first convention held to discuss the rights of women

   _____

4. the name of the compromise that divided the United States into free states and slave states

   _____

5. the name of the new country formed by the states that had seceded from the Union

   _____

   _____

6. the name of the compromise that allowed California to be admitted to the United States as a free state

   _____

7. allowed Kansas and Nebraska to decide for themselves whether or not to allow slavery

   _____

8. someone who wanted to end slavery in the United States

   _____

9. the idea that each state should be allowed to make its own decisions

   _____

10. the system of secret routes that escaping enslaved people followed to freedom

    _____

11. required police in free states to help capture escaping enslaved people

    _____

THE CIVIL WAR BEGINS

Use the map below to help you complete the activities. For help, you can refer to pages 472–477 in your textbook.

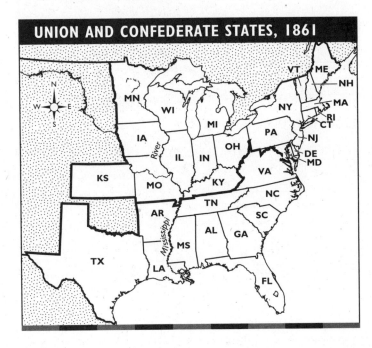

UNION AND CONFEDERATE STATES, 1861

1. Color the Union states on the map blue. Color the Confederate states gray.

2. What were the three parts of the Union's Anaconda Plan for victory?

   _____

   _____

   _____

3. Circle in red the state where the first battle of the Civil War occurred.

4. Circle in black the state that was the site of the First Battle of Bull Run. Who won this battle?

   _____

THE WAR TAKES A NEW DIRECTION

Use the words and pictures to help you complete the activities on this page. For help, you can refer to pages 478–485 in your textbook.

1. The name of this document is . . .

_____

_____

2. What did this document do?

_____

_____

_____

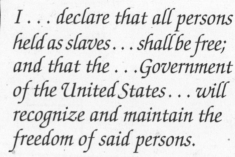

I . . . declare that all persons held as slaves . . . shall be free; and that the . . . Government of the United States . . . will recognize and maintain the freedom of said persons.

EMANCIPATION PROCLAMATION

3. How did this document change the way people felt about the war?

_____

_____

4. Read these words from a famous speech made by President Lincoln. Which battle is he referring to?

_____

5. How did this battle affect the course of the war?

_____

_____

_____

Now we are engaged in a great civil war, testing whether that nation, or any nation so conceived and so dedicated, can long endure. We are met on a great battlefield of that war. We have come to dedicate a portion of that field as a final resting place for those who here gave their lives that that nation might live. It is altogether fitting and proper that we should do this.

GETTYSBURG ADDRESS

6. What did President Lincoln's speech make clear about the war?

_____

_____

_____

MAKING GENERALIZATIONS

Read the information in the chart. Then complete the activities below. For help, you can refer to pages 486–487 in your textbook.

FACTS ABOUT FOUR CIVIL WAR GENERALS			
GRANT	**MEADE**	**LEE**	**JACKSON**
attended the U.S. Military Academy	attended the U.S. Military Academy	attended the U.S. Military Academy	attended the U.S. Military Academy
had experience in the Mexican War	had experience in the Mexican War	had experience in the Mexican War	had experience in the Mexican War
had the respect of his soldiers	had the respect of his soldiers	had the respect of his soldiers	had the respect of his soldiers
sudden changes didn't affect him	was considered tough and reliable	took chances others wouldn't take	was able to plan a strong defense
believed in quick, decisive action.	believed in quick, decisive action	believed in quick, decisive action	believed in quick, decisive action
put in charge of the entire Union army	was known for his quick temper	stopped the Union army in Virginia	paid careful attention to military detail

1. What three generalizations could you make from the information in the chart? Circle the letter next to each one.

    a. Most Civil War generals had military training and experience.

    b. Most Civil War generals are known for their quick temper.

    c. Most Civil War generals are respected by their soldiers.

    d. Most Civil War generals believed in quick, decisive action.

    e. Most Civil War generals pay careful attention to military detail.

2. How did you decide on your answers to the first question?

_____

_____

3. Why is it useful to be able to make generalizations about a topic?

_____

_____

McGraw-Hill School Division

THINKING ABOUT THE END OF THE CIVIL WAR

Use the map to help you complete the activities below. For help, you can refer to pages 488–493 in your textbook.

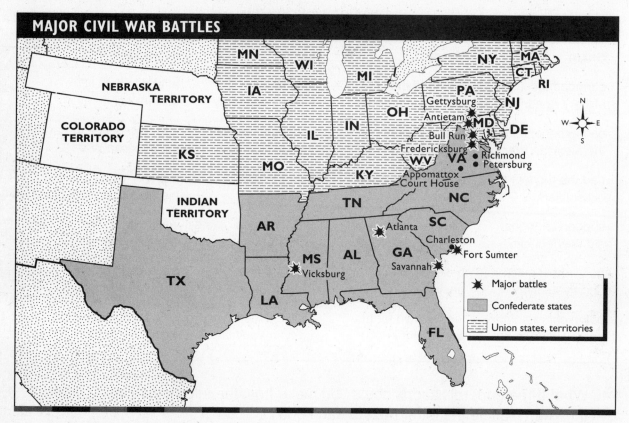

MAJOR CIVIL WAR BATTLES

Legend:
- ✸ Major battles
- ▨ Confederate states
- ▦ Union states, territories

1. Draw in red the route General Sherman took on his march through Georgia.

2. What did Sherman want to achieve by waging total war on the South?

_____

_____

3. Circle the two cities that Grant's men entered and captured.

4. Why had General Lee left these cities?

_____

_____

5. Put an **X** on the place where Lee surrendered to Grant.

Why did Lee surrender?

_____

_____

_____

6. How had the war changed the South?

_____

_____

_____

McGraw-Hill School Division

THINKING ABOUT RECONSTRUCTION

Read the statements below. If a statement is true, write **True** after it. If a statement is false, write **False** after it. In the space provided, write the reasons for your answer. For help, refer to pages 494–498 in your textbook.

1. The Thirteenth, Fourteenth, and Fifteenth amendments extended the rights of African Americans.

   _____

   _____

   _____

2. President Johnson carried out President Lincoln's plan for Reconstruction.

   _____

   _____

   _____

   _____

3. Congress wanted President Johnson to end Reconstruction. _____

   _____

   _____

   _____

4. Congress created the Freedmen's Bureau to help African Americans after the Civil War.

   _____

   _____

5. Under Reconstruction, African American men were not able to vote.

   _____

   _____

McGraw-Hill School Division

MATCHING WORDS AND THEIR MEANINGS

Write the letter of each term next to its meaning. For help, you can refer
to the lessons in Chapter 17 of your textbook.

a. total war   f. segregation   j. Freedmen's Bureau   n. Thirteenth Amendment

b. blockade   g. sharecropping   k. Anaconda Plan   o. Fourteenth Amendment

c. impeach   h. Jim Crow laws   l. Reconstruction   p. Emancipation Proclamation

d. Civil War   i. Ku Klux Klan   m. Gettysburg Address   q. Fifteenth Amendment

e. black codes

_____ 1. the system of renting land for a share of the crop raised on the land

_____ 2. abolishes slavery

_____ 3. to block off

_____ 4. Southern laws that described the rights and duties of freed African Americans

_____ 5. the announcement that ended slavery in the Confederacy

_____ 6. the separation of white people and black people

_____ 7. a group of Southerners formed to frighten and control African Americans and their white supporters

_____ 8. a famous speech by President Lincoln

_____ 9. gives all male citizens of the United States the right to vote, regardless of race

_____ 10. rebuilding the South

_____ 11. the Union's plan for victory in the Civil War

_____ 12. an agency established by Congress to help African Americans after the Civil War

_____ 13. the war between the Southern states and the Northern states

_____ 14. makes African Americans citizens of the United States and guarantees them the same legal rights as whites

_____ 15. to charge a government official with wrongdoing

_____ 16. an all-out war to destroy people's ability and will to fight

_____ 17. laws that made discrimination against African Americans legal

McGraw-Hill School Division

TABLE OF CONTENTS

McGraw-Hill School Division

Name: Date:

Create a Classroom Collage

Complete each sentence.

• This collage makes me feel

_____

_____

• One place on the collage I'd like to visit is

_____

_____

• The people in the collage are different because

_____

_____

_____

_____

• The people in the collage are alike because

_____

_____

_____

_____

_____

McGraw-Hill School Division

Present a T.V. Talk Show

Write questions in the blanks that you will ask during the T.V. Talk Show.
Remember: Who, What, When, Where, Why.

_____

_____

_____

_____

_____

_____

_____

_____

_____

NOTES _____

_____

_____

_____

_____

_____

McGraw-Hill School Division

Make a History Picture Time Line

Color, cut out, and attach each arrow to the bottom of each picture. Then write in the date.

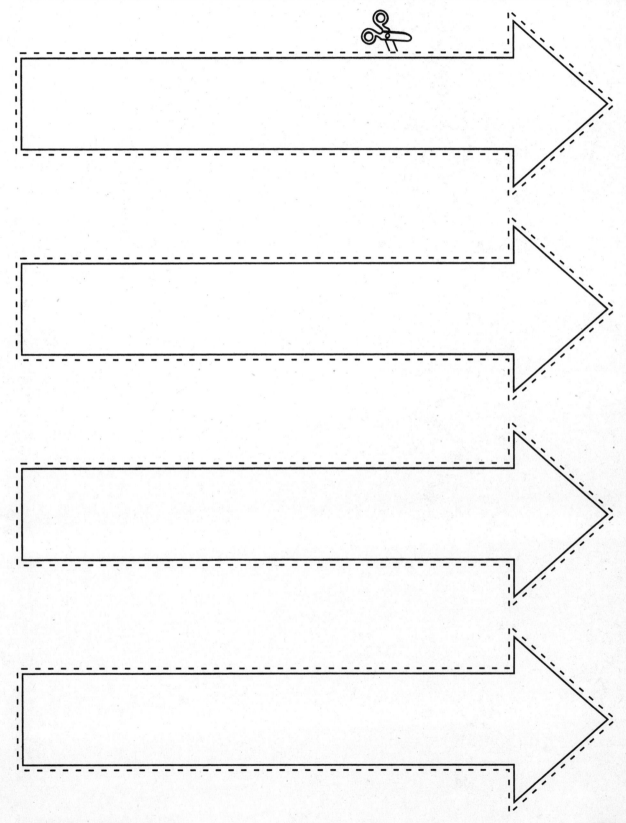

Put on a Play

Fill in the chart to plan your play.

WHO is in the scene?	WHAT is happening?	WHERE does the action take place?

McGraw-Hill School Division

Show Headlines from History

Write your headline in the top part of the page and then draw your front page photo from history below it.

THE DAILY GLOBE

McGraw-Hill School Division

Produce a Movie

Decorate and fill in the poster to advertise your movie.

NOW SHOWING:

_____

NARRATED BY:

_____

ANIMATED BY:

_____

_____

Put Together a Song Album

Fill in the blanks to complete your Table of Contents and then decorate the margins.

Table of Contents

Songs I listened to: _____

_____

_____

Songs I adapted: _____

_____

_____

Songs I made up: _____

_____

_____

_____

Why I liked listening to the songs: _____

_____

_____

_____

_____

_____

_____

McGraw-Hill School Division